HISTORY'S LAST STAND

HISTORY'S LAST STAND

GERARD

AND

PATRICIA DEL RE

AVON BOOKS ◆ NEW YORK

AVON BOOKS
A division of
The Hearst Corporation
1350 Avenue of the Americas
New York, New York 10019

Copyright © 1993 by Gerard Del Re and Patricia Del Re
Cover art by Tracy Britt
Published by arrangement with the authors
Library of Congress Catalog Card Number: 92-97444
ISBN: 0-380-76915-8

First Avon Books Trade Printing: June 1993

AVON TRADEMARK REG. U.S. PAT. OFF. AND IN OTHER COUNTRIES, MARCA REGISTRADA, HECHO EN U.S.A

Printed in the U.S.A.

OPM 10 9 8 7 6 5 4 3 2 1

This Book is Dedicated to
Barbara S. Kouts

Acknowledgments

We would like to express our immense gratitude to Bill Bindy, Ralph Burger, Al Golub, Arthur Martinson, M. Lovette Pollock, and Marlyne Tannen for their encouragement.

A very special thanks to Mim L. Pollock for her many kindnesses.

*I know of no other way
of judging the future
but by the past.*

PATRICK HENRY

A Note on the Format

The chronological listing is designed to serve the reader by offering a point of reference. Listing the events in the order in which they occurred allows the reader to see how events might relate to one another and gives the book a sense of order. Through the chronological format we observe the flow of time as it relates not only to history but often to ourselves as well.

Introduction

In this age of information when new events dot our horizons daily, somehow vital historical facts surrounding events a thousand years ago—like when a famous war ended and who fought whom—have been forgotten. Often high school students or people on the street, when queried about the past, be it the causes of a war, a president's term of office, the meaning and significance of a holiday, seem to know or remember nothing. George Santayana's admonition, "Those who cannot remember the past are condemned to repeat it," appears to have some merit. World War II was the result of learning too few lessons from World War I. Certainly, the captain of the ocean liner *Titanic* had been schooled in the hazards of the North Atlantic, but chose to forget his honorable duty in a quest to accomplish a speed record. Perhaps it is human to forget, even to ignore the past, particularly with our burdensome, hurried lives in this supertechnological age of windowless buildings, cellular phones, word processors, and organ transplants.

With science and math becoming dominant forces in the academic world, with history finding fewer slots in college curriculums, those who know their history are often perceived to hold the keys to extraordinary secrets. But history is not for the chosen few. Rather, it is vital to all of us because it can teach us, give us real examples of potential mistakes. It took the death of several presidents by assassination to make us understand the necessity of protecting the person chosen for the Oval Office. After the peace of World War II, instead of demanding exorbitant indemnities from Germany, as we did after World War I, we helped that country rebuild with the Marshall Plan. We also helped Japan rebuild.Today both countries add to everyone's quality of life. And so it goes.

History's Last Stand is not meant to be a textbook but rather a reference work that one can enjoy reading. There are no question-and-answer sections. We have tried to capture the drama, the intensity and vividness of an event, while sticking to the facts at the same time. Of course, we could not have hoped to cover every event and person in history—that task would be impossible given our limited space. But we believe these accounts of events and people will give readers a sense of the importance and the benefit of remembering the past.

GERARD AND PATRICIA DEL RE

HISTORY'S
LAST
STAND

PELOPONNESIAN WARS

Last Day: On April 25, 404 B.C., Athens surrendered to Sparta after its food supply was cut off.

Background: Both Athens and Sparta were rivals for the leadership of Greece, and Athenian imperialism earned Sparta's hatred. The first of the Peloponnesian Wars began in 432 B.C. with a revolt by the Potidaea in the spring. The death of the great Athenian leader and statesman Pericles from plague in the autumn of 429 B.C. signaled the end of the Golden Age of Greece—a period of great progress and prosperity—and robbed Athens of the one figure who most embodied her hope and survival.

Sparta, a mighty power, was soon to triumph over Athenian sea power at the Battle of Syracuse, in spite of the Athenian armada of over 150 warships. The famous battle was the beginning of the demise of Athenian power and influence. On the fateful day April 25, 404 B.C., the sound of Spartan flutes signaled the call to battle that would bring down Athens's Long Walls, and her glory was gone forever.

NEKHTNEBF DYNASTY

Last Native Dynasty of Ancient Egypt: The Nekhtnebf Dynasty, the thirtieth of the dynasties of old Egypt, which began in 405 B.C., ended in 332 B.C.

Background: The Nekhtnebf House did not have the splendor of Egypt's most significant dynasty, the eighteenth New Empire Kingdom (1570–1342 B.C.) from which came King Tutankhamen, popularly known as King Tut. But it *was* distinguished because it was the last. In 332 B.C. Alexander the Great conquered Egypt, ending the dynasties of old. Egyptian kings were called pharaohs and had ruled since 2300 B.C. and the days of Menes.

ACHAEMENID DYNASTY

Last Day: On October 1, 331 B.C., Alexander of Macedon triumphed over Darius III in the Battle of Gaugamela in Mesopotamia, ending two centuries of rule by Persian kings. The victory gained Alexander the title Alexander the Great and made him ruler of the Persian Empire.

Background: The dynasty of Persian kings, the Achaemenid dynasty was founded by King Cyrus the Great in 550 B.C. Alexander the Great, after eventual victories in northern India, defeating Porus on the Hydaspes and becoming one of the greatest conquerers the world would see, died of a fever on May 18, 323 B.C., at age thirty-two.

ALEXANDER THE GREAT

Last Day of Life: On May 18, 323 B.C., Alexander the Great, the Macedonian king, died at Babylon after a prolonged fever, the exact cause of death unknown. Before being taken ill, Alexander had attended a banquet. Within six months of his death, rumors began to circulate that the great leader had been poisoned. Born in 356 B.C., he was thirty-two years old.

Background: Alexander the Great lived a short thirty-two years, but few military leaders could ever have dreamed of conquering so much. Known also as Alexander III, he was tutored by Aristotle as a child. Upon the murder of his father, Alexander (who had no hand in his demise) came to the throne and began his brilliant career as a soldier by calming the belligerent cities of Greece and putting down uprisings in such cities as Trace and Illyria. When it heard a rumor that he had been killed, the city of Thebes revolted. Alexander rushed upon the city, razing its buildings but not its temples.

In 334 B.C., with Greece and the Balkans under his control, Alexander conquered Persia, a country whose armies were previously considered invincible. Syria was next, after which fell Egypt in 332 B.C. In 330 B.C., discovering a plot to assassinate him, Alexander infuriated his soldiers when he executed not only a general's son who was implicated in the plot, but also the innocent general. In 327 B.C. Alexander invaded Italy and attained some victories, but his men wanted no more of war. In 324 B.C. his army returned to Persia. He founded the city of Alexandria on the banks of the Mediterranean in 332 B.C. At the time of his death, Alexander the Great had extended the Hellenistic world to India's borders. Such conquests spread Greek civilization throughout the ancient world.

BATTLE OF ZAMA

Last Day: The second Punic War ended in the downfall of Hannibal, Carthaginian warrior and statesman, on October 19, 202 B.C.

Background: The Battle of Zama (sometimes rendered as Sama), pitted Hannibal against Roman forces commanded by General Scipio Africanus. At Zama, in North Africa and southwest of Carthage, Roman forces fought with determination to obliterate the faithless Carthaginians. Facing the heavily armed ranks of Carthaginians and Numidians, Hannibal's army folded before the skilled Roman legionnaires. Hannibal is perhaps best remembered for driving an elephant caravan across the Alps, which forged a route later used by the Romans at Cannes who escaped to Bithynia (old name for Turkey).

Later, pursued by Rome, Hannibal took poison to end his life in 183 B.C. after feeling betrayed by his host, King Prusias. Rome destroyed Carthage once and for all in 146 B.C. in the third and Last Punic War, pouring salt in the furrows of its soil and plowing it under.

JULIUS CAESAR

Last Day of Life: Julius Caesar was stabbed to death by conspirators on March 15, 44 B.C.

Background: Julius Caesar's rule had become too autocratic; some thought and even went so far as to suggest that he take the title king. His enemies were infuriated, by his behavior, as they were mostly highborn Romans who preferred to place their trust in the country at large rather than in one man.

The conspiracy to slay Caesar involved some sixty individuals, and the last element to be decided upon was the place of the assassination. The principals of the plot were Gaius Cassius, Marcus Brutus, and Decimus Brutus. After some bickering, the place was chosen: the Pompeian Assembly Room. The day would be the Ides of March—fifteenth day of March. The year was 44 B.C. The city, Rome.

On the day of Julius Caesar's death, one of the plotters began to have second thoughts about carrying out the deed. As the Roman ruler was on his way to meet with the Senate, a cryptic note was passed to him. But Caesar was too preoccupied with keeping his appointment with the august Roman assembly to give the note his attention and simply allowed it to become lost with other papers in his hand.

Upon entering the Senate near noon, Caesar repaired to the Pompeian Assembly Room, where he was escorted to the chair-of-state by Marcus Brutus. Caesar had no sooner been seated when a mass of men, led by Tillius Cimber, besieged him. Cimber grabbed at Caesar's purple robes, grasping his shoulder. Caesar, shocked by such a breach of conduct cried, "This is violence!" A blade struck just below his throat, the first wound inflicted. Caesar grabbed the arm of the perpetrator and stabbed him with his stylus. Rising up from his chair Caesar was struck with another dagger, this one tearing into his breast. But Caesar remained on his feet, where he fell victim to a raging shower of daggers, twenty-three thrusts all told. The sight of one of his assailants shocked Caesar. "You too, my son" to Marcus Brutus, groaned the dictator. Pulling his purple bloodstained toga over his face, Caesar collapsed, dead near the statue of Pompey. He was fifty years old.

BATTLE OF ACTIUM

Last Day: On September 2, 31 B.C., a naval battle called the Battle of Actium took place at the entrance of the Ambracian Gulf between Roman forces and soldiers loyal to Cleopatra, led by Marcus Antonius.

Background: The Battle of Ac⁺ium resulted from the feuding of two Roman leaders, Octavian (the future Caesar Augustus) and his rival in popularity, Marcus Antonius (Marc Anthony). Antonius, while still legally married to Octavian's sister, wed Cleopatra VII, whose beauty he could not resist. Given the eastern lands of the Roman Empire after the empire was cut into three parts on the death of Julius Caesar, Antonius transferred Roman territory to his ambitious Egyptian bride. The relationship between Octavian and Antonius, always tenuous, collapsed with Antonius's marriage to the Egyptian queen.

Octavian drew first blood by airing before the Roman Senate a will, whose information was supposed to be privileged. Though some suspected that part of the information was forged, the will disclosed that Antonius had bequeathed Roman lands to the queen. Fearing that Cleopatra's ambition might exceed the boundaries of the East, the Roman Senate declared war on the queen. Octavian also felt that Rome would never have peace until Antonius was gone.

The naval battle at Actium went poorly for Antonius because his soldiers, some forty thousand against Octavian's thirty-eight thousand legionnaires, deserted him. Octavian spent the night of the battle in his flagship receiving glowing reports of the drawn-out battle from his commanders. Antonius simply was not the leader that Octavian was. Antonius sued for peace, but Octavian ordered him to commit suicide, which he did. Octavian rose to become Caesar Augustus in 27 B.C., giving Rome a period of peace known as the Pax Romana.

CLEOPATRA VII

Last Day of Life: The last of the Cleopatras was Cleopatra VII, whose beauty was legendary. On August 12 or thereabouts in the year 30 B.C., distraught over the defeat of her Roman lover, Marcus Antonius (Marc Anthony) at the Battle of Actium at the hands of Octavian, the Egyptian queen ended her life by swallowing poison that she kept in a hollow ornamental hairpin. Another cause of

Cleopatra's death is put forth by Plutarch, who believed a serpent was responsible for the famous queen's death, though no serpent was found when Roman soldiers arrived at the dead queen's palace.

Background: Cleopatra's mother was Cleopatra VI Tryphaena, and her father was Ptolemy XI. Cleopatra VII ruled Egypt with her brother, Ptolemy XII (61?–47 B.C.), who was also her husband until he banished her from his palace. With the aid of Rome, and Julius Caesar in particular, Cleopatra dethroned her husband, who later drowned while fleeing Caesar's army. The scheming queen managed to keep the Ptolemy Dynasty alive by marrying Ptolemy XIII (58?–44 B.C.), a younger brother, while at the same time becoming mistress to Julius Caesar—taking up residence at his palace on the Palatine Hill in Rome.

   Having given Julius Caesar a son, Caesarion, Queen Cleopatra returned to Egypt after Caesar's assassination in 44 B.C. There she had her husband murdered so that Caesarion might share her Egyptian throne in joint rule. Caesarion, who later became Ptolemy XIV (47–30 B.C.), was murdered at Augustus's order after Cleopatra's death. In 42 B.C. Cleopatra was visited by Marcus Antonius on behalf of Octavian. The handsome and flamboyant Roman fell under the queen's spell, and though still married to Octavian's sister, he nevertheless married Cleopatra in 36 B.C., thus incurring the wrath of the future emperor. In 31 B.C. Antonius took up arms against Octavian in the Battle of Actium, and lost. He committed suicide. When she received word of Antonius's death and of Octavian's intention to parade her before the eyes of Rome as his trophy, Cleopatra VII took her life. Born in 69 B.C., she was thirty-nine years old.

CAESAR AUGUSTUS

Last Day of Life: The first Roman emperor, Caesar Augustus, died on August 19, A.D. 14.

Background: Roman's mightest emperor, Caesar Augustus, filled his last days in A.D. 14 closing out a world census. With his stepson, Tiberius Caesar, chosen as his successor, Augustus was ready to bid the world goodbye at age seventy-six. He could look back over his life and be proud of his accomplishments, among them having added Egypt to Rome's possessions and giving rise to an Augustine Age, a period when arts and letters were encouraged and rewarded. At Nola, with his wife, Livia, Augustus was made comfortable in the family villa. On the nineteenth of August—his good-luck month—he passed the day in the private company of Livia, who stroked his thin white hair and kissed his aged, wise face. Augustus looked into his beloved's eyes, murmuring, "Farewell, Livia, live mindful of our marriage." Moments later, in her arms Caesar Augustus slipped away. The cause of death was old age. He was born in 63 B.C.

Caesar Augustus, originally known as Octavian, was the first and greatest Roman emperor. The grand-nephew of Julius Caesar, Augustus came to power at a very uneasy time in Roman history. With the death of Julius Caesar by assassination in 44 B.C., Augustus, after dispatching the murderers, in 43 B.C. formed a triumvirate sharing the power of authority over the empire with Marcus Antonius and Lepidus. Augustus began his ascendency to eventual sole control of the Roman Empire when Lepidus become involved in distant Sicily in 36 B.C., and Antonius fell to Augustus at the naval Battle of Actium in 31 B.C. Antonius committed suicide and Lepidus was placed in captivity.

In 27 B.C. Augustus made himself emperor of the Roman Empire. This empire would eventually extend beyond the walls of Rome, spanning two and a half million square miles from the River Euphrates in Asia to the coast of Spain, from the vast regions of Africa's Sahara all the way to Great Britain, while embracing one hundred million people.

Augustus's reign was a glorious one, a period that become known as the Pax Romana, or Roman Peace. Under Augustus the empire enjoyed good government, many fine public works were instituted, just laws to protect slaves were enacted, and safe sea and overland travel prevailed throughout most of the empire. To guard the

Pax Romana, Rome had a massive army consisting of thirty-three legions, about two hundred thousand soldiers. Augustus's name arises annually throughout the world at Christmas as Christians hear one of the most famous sentences in the Bible concerning the birth of Christ: "And it came to pass in those days, that there went out a decree from Caesar Augustus, that all the world should be taxed . . . " (Luke 2:1).

LAST SUPPER

Last Meal of Christ: The Last Supper (see Matthew 26: 1–29) was the Passover meal taken by Christ with His twelve apostles on Holy Thursday in approximately A.D. 33.

Background: At the Passover meal Christ instituted the Holy Eucharist and foretold his betrayal by one among the twelve. *The Last Supper* is also the title of numerous art depictions of this meal, the most famous of which is probably the painting by the Florentine artist Leonardo da Vinci, created in 1497. Da Vinci's *Last Supper* depicts the moment during the meal when the apostles asked "Lord, is it I?" in response to Christ's disclosure that one in their midst would betray him. Painted on the refectory wall of the Dominican Convent, Santa Maria Grazie, Milan, Italy, the painting has suffered much deterioration, a condition that began even while the artist lived. Noticeable in da Vinci's rendering of the mystical meal is the absence of Christ's chalice.

HEALING OF MALCHUS

Last Miracle by Christ Before His Death on the Cross: On the night of Holy Thursday, in approximately A.D. 33 as he was being arrested in the Garden of Olives, Jesus healed the severed ear of Malchus, the servant of the high priest.

Background: While Jesus was speaking to his disciples, a crowd appeared, and Judas, one of Christ's twelve apostles, led the high priests and Roman soldiers to Jesus, identifying him with a kiss. Jesus said, "Judas, betrayest thou the Son of Man with a kiss?" As the priests and soldiers moved upon Jesus, Peter, one of Christ's disciples broke forth, drew his sword from its scabbard, and cut off the ear of the servant Malchus. Jesus ordered Peter to put down his sword. He touched the servant's wound and he was made whole. (Luke 22:47–52; John 18:10)

PTOLEMY OF MAURETANIA

Last of the Ptolemies: The last Ptolemy was King Ptolemy of Mauretania, son of Jube II (king of Numidia) and Cleopatra Selene V; he was executed in A.D. 40.

Background: King Ptolemy of Mauretania was a cousin of the mad Roman emperor Caligula. Invited to Rome by the emperor, the handsome Ptolemy, with his shock of abundant hair—of which the bald Caligula was jealous—made a fatal mistake. He offended the emperor's excessive vanity by appearing in the royal box at a Roman amphitheater attired in purple robes that drew the admiration of the masses. The enraged Caligula had the king secretly executed in A.D. 40, thus ending the powerful Egyptian dynasty.

The Ptolemies brought forth through marriage the queen and princesses known by the name Cleopatra—seven in all. Through wisely calculated marriages and accomplishments on the battlefields of Egypt and Libya in defense of these lands, Ptolemy I rose in power and a dynasty was born. Making Alexandria, Egypt, his capital, Ptolemy I lived a long life, passing his kingdom on to his son, Ptolemy II, or Ptolemy Philadelphus (309–246 B.C.). Other Ptolemies included Ptolemy VI, king from 181 to 145 B.C., who married his own sister, Cleopatra II; and Ptolemy XII, who died in a drowning accident while fleeing the armies of Julius Caesar in 49 B.C., and was married to the Cleopatra of legendary beauty, the seventh of the Cleopatras. The Ptolemies continued during the reign of Roman Emperor Caligula (A.D. 37–41) ending with the death of Ptolemy of Mauretania.

CALIGULA

Last Day of Life: Caligula, emperor of Rome, also called Gaius Caesar, was assassinated on January 24, A.D. 41.

Background: Popular discontent with Emperor Caligula had reached its peak, and rumors of assassination were in the wind. On January 24, A.D. 41, Caligula, with his German guard out of range, stopped to watch a theater group rehearsing a Greek dance in Rome. Caligula needed the distraction to relieve a stomachache after banqueting the previous night. Responding to a question, Caligula uttered the word "Jupiter." The next instant a club landed across the emperor's jaw, causing him to fall to the ground in pain. As the dying emperor taunted his assassins with "I am still alive. Strike again," a ring of sword-carrying attackers closed in on him with a vengeance, ending Caligula's life at age twenty-eight.

The Roman Empire emerged from the stormy period of the Republic, having buried Carthage, stopped Spartacus, and set the world on a stable course, and now what was known as the empire period began—so named because emperors ruled the world. Caesar Augustus in 27 B.C. was first after he had purged Rome of its enemies—those who had killed Julius Caesar in 44 B.C. With Augustus's death on August 19, A.D. 14, his stepson Tiberius Caesar was chosen to succeed him. Rome prospered under Tiberius and when he died on March 16, A.D. 37, the Roman treasury was 680 million gold pieces wealthier. But Tiberius in his final years of life had grown cynical, depraved, and cruel, and held contempt for the office of emperor. He sought to leave Rome with something to remember him by. He chose as his successor his inexperienced, unstable, and sadistic nephew Gaius Caesar, nicknamed Bootikin or Little Boots.

Gaius Caesar Caligula was twenty-six when he became

ruler of the world. To Caligula, the Roman Empire was a toy to be played with. He had little respect for his position, instead using his station to raid the Roman treasury of most of its wealth, squandering it within a year of his reign. He once said, "Let them [the Roman people] hate me, so long as they fear me." Caligula sickened the Roman nobility with his cruelty, which included the feeding of slaves to his twelve lions when animals used for food were in short supply. He had citizens killed for the smallest infractions—failing to smile, being unable to guess what he was thinking. He liked to fill the arena with old, infirm people and criminals who would battle to the death with swords to excite his passion for blood. Banquets were times for orgies, where the vilest indecencies were committed. Failure to please at such times might result in a knight having his head lopped off in the presence of other guests. Citizens often had to go without food when, on a whim, Caligula had the granaries closed. He laughed at mobs in the streets or stadiums who shrieked with anger over their miserable living conditions. When he grew tired of these screaming masses, he set the Praetorian guards on them, laughing even more as the guards beat them to death. With no money left in the Roman treasury to feed his insatiable appetite for pleasure, Caligula raised additional funds by stealing private property, demanding gifts from nobles and their inheritances in the name of the state.

The emperor almost caused a full-scale war in Judea when he sought to have a statue of himself erected in the Temple of Jerusalem. It did incite a riot, and only the wise prevailings of the Syrian legate Petronius prevented a bloodbath. To protect himself from bodily harm, Caligula employed a fiercely loyal German guard named Chaerea. His personal bodyguards were so blindly loyal that the emperor need only wink to signal a command, and in a flash a subject might be murdered on the spot, the clothes from his back grabbed, or a throng decimated, usually for nothing more than the emperor's whim.

NERO

Last Day of Life: Nero, emperor of Rome, also called Claudius Augustus Germanicus, committed suicide on June 9, A.D. 68.

Background: Rome was at its lowest point in June A.D. 68, with extreme poverty, high crime, and famine sending the city into near collapse. Clearly, something had to be done. Nero was not a man of wisdom, but in fact he was rather naive. His enemies hatched a plot to deceive the emperor by telling him that the Senate had condemned him to death, and suicide was the only alternative left to him. Believing that the Roman army had deserted him, Nero fled and spent his final hours hiding in a villa on the northern edge of Rome.

Tortured by the belief that he would be publicly humiliated, and paraded naked before the public of Rome if he did not take his life, Nero, on June 9, A.D. 68, was ready to commit suicide. In the presence of some close friends, Nero, weeping, put a dagger to his throat and with the aid of one of his companions, pushed the blade into his flesh. He lingered near death for less than an hour. When a Roman centurion came upon the scene and attempted to administer aid, Nero said his last words: "Too late. How loyal you are." Nero, the last of the Caesarian line was dead at age thirty.

With the death of the feeble Roman emperor, Claudius, (October 13, A.D. 54), at age sixty-three, murdered with poison by his wife Agrippina, her son Nero became emperor of the Roman Empire. Nero was sixteen years old. After Caesar Augustus, Nero is the most famous Roman emperor. He was the only emperor who aspired to be an artist, quite capable of playing the lyre. Nero also wrote poetry, and believed he sang well, but his admirers were merely stroking his vanity out of fear for their lives.

Nero suffered from several human excesses, among these a great love of food. He also had enormous sexual drives and among his sexual partners were his mother, whom he had executed, men, women, and even children. Strangely, Nero is supposed to have cringed at the sight of blood, yet Saints Peter and Paul were martyred during his reign. One must also remember Nero persecuted the first Christians, sending many to the wild beasts in the arena.

When discontent raised its furious head, the emperor cut if off, having many Roman nobles assassinated. Under Nero's reign, taxes were raised to support his pet projects, among these a fancy edifice called the Golden House, an illustrious palace created for his pleasure. After his death, the palace was torn down to make way for the great stadium called the Colosseum. Nero was not happy with the way Rome was laid out and sought to reconstruct the city. When a fire broke out on July 19, A.D. 63, in the vicinity of the great Circus Maximus and swept over the Palatine Hill where the emperors lived, and destroyed many state buildings, Nero became the scapegoat. His enemies circulated unfounded rumors that he had ordered the fire set, and that he had even been seen playing his lyre (not a fiddle as legend has it, since the violin would not be invented for another ten centuries). If anything, Nero wept, for he loved Rome and only sought to improve its streets, squares, and waterfronts.

POMPEII

Last Day: The pleasure resort city and Roman port in Italy was totally destroyed under tons of mud, volcanic ash, and lava after Mount Vesuvius erupted on August 24, A.D. 79, sending devastating tremors through the region and spewing white-hot flames thousands of feet into the air.

Background: Mount Vesuvius erupted during business hours after simmering for some days with light smoke, dust, and bits of cinder. Pompeii at the time was involved in a massive reconstruction program after having suffered a severe earthquake some sixteen years before in A.D. 63.

August 24 was a rainy day, and the air thickened with noxious fumes that made breathing difficult. Then suddenly a series of ear-shattering explosions caused the ground to shake violently and with such force that Pompeii and the neighboring city of Herculaneum began to crumble under the turbulence. Day changed to night and the air, heavy with ash and pumice stone, became noticeably warm.

Rivers of lava descended from Mount Vesuvius's crater, slowly inching toward the city. The lava crushed walls, swept away trees and houses, and destroyed boats and the city's docks, thus trapping the throngs. Thousands of people, quickly exhausted from the lack of oxygen, suffocated to death, while others fell victim to the heat, were trampled to death, or were burned alive by the rivers of lava. Some were victims of falling houses and trees. Others were buried alive under the weight of the mud in which they became bogged down. Estimates of the death toll range from two thousand to twenty thousand citizens, among them many of Italy's wealthiest people, for the Caesars, Roman senators, consuls, and business merchants vacationed at Pompeii.

On April 1, 1748, excavations based on the geographic writings of the Roman Pliny the Younger led to the unearthing of Pompeii. Pompeii was a city active in civic affairs, one of the great cultural centers of the Roman Empire, with the fine arts—painting, sculpture, literature, and theater—as well as sports prominent in its daily life.

HEROD AGRIPPA II

Last of the Herods: Herod Agrippa II (Marcus Julius), son of Herod Agrippa I; Agrippa II died in A.D. 100.

Background: Agrippa II reigned by the good graces of Rome in A.D. 52 at the time of the Christian era, ruling in northern Palestine. He was not a good ruler, having the excesses of character associated with all the Herods, notably ambition. A bully, Agrippa II overplayed his importance. Saint Paul appeared before him, as is recorded in the Acts of the Apostles, where Agrippa II is referred to as a king. He died in A.D. 100, after retiring to Rome.

Other Herods include Herod the Great, whose reign began in 34 B.C. Herod the Great was made a king by the Roman Senate. He had the babies of Bethlehem killed after the Magi failed to return to Jerusalem with news of the Christ Child's whereabouts. He also built the beautiful Temple of Jerusalem and whole cities, earning him the title Herod the Builder. There were also Herod Archelaus, an ineffective ruler; Herod Antipas, who had John the Baptist beheaded, and before whom Christ appeared during his trial; Herod Philip, a tetrarch of Batanea and the Dan region, who was the mildest of the Herods; Herod of Chalcis, brother of Agrippa I, who ruled Chalcis, north of Galilee; and Herod Agrippa I, friend of the Emperor Claudius.

GLADIATORIAL SPECTACLES OF ANCIENT ROME

Last Day: On January 1, 404, the gladiator sporting events were over after the monk Telemachus was brutally murdered while attempting to separate two combating gladiators in the Colosseum in Rome. Telemachus' death at the hands of an enraged mob caused the Emperor Flavius Honorius officially to abolish the age-old Roman cult of the gladiatoral contests forever. He had abolished the gladiator schools throughout Rome in 399.

Background: The games of blood and gore had had their place in Roman life since Romulus founded Rome in 753 B.C. The Etruscans (the predecessors of the Ancient Romans) believed that the dead were in pain and agony over their loss of life and that the way to appease their spirits was to offer sacrifices—not of animals, but of men. Hence the cult of the gladiator was born.

ROMAN-HUNNISH BATTLE OF CHALONS

Last Day: On September 20, 451, the Huns, fierce Asiatic barbarian warrior tribes led by Attila, the Scourge of God, fell to Roman and Visigoth forces under the command of Flavius Aetius and Theodoric I, at the Battle of Chalons-sur-Marne, France.

Background: The Battle of Chalons-sur-Marne was one of the few defeats for the mighty Attila, whose army numbered over forty thousand men, most on horseback. The Huns lost the battle in what was a retreat back across the Rhine, with thousands killed on both sides. Until Chalons, Attila had seemed invincible. Attila and his barbarians, whose standard was a skull with horns, first appeared on the Italian scene in about 406. With various crude arms, dressed in the hides of animals, and wearing horned helmets, Attila and his men were expert horsemen. Seemingly unstoppable, they stormed across central Europe, overrunning towns, laying siege to cities large and small, and annihilating people with unspeakable savagery, while extracting gold, grain, and livestock as tribute. The mighty Attila swept across the Balkans, conquering those nations before invading Gaul, leaving so much death and destruction in his wake that he and his Huns were likened to plagues, with the bloody leader earning the black title the Scourge of God.

It seemed that only the power of Almighty God could diffuse this human catastrophe. In 452, his army having burst upon the Alps, Attila was ready to rampage through Rome when he agreed to meet with Pope Leo I, the Great, on the banks of Mincio River. Prevailing upon Attila for mercy and warning of the wrath of God, the pope succeeded in persuading the Hunnish king to turn away from Rome. Attila was found dead in 453 after his soldiers broke into his chambers when he failed to appear before his army at noon after a night of feasting. The infamous Attila had suffocated during a hemorrhaging of the nose.

ROMAN EMPIRE (WEST)

Last Day: On August 28, 476, the child emperor Romulus Augustus was deposed by Odoacer, a Saxon ruler. The period known as the Middle Ages began after Augustus was removed.

Background: Twenty-one years before the fall of the Roman Empire, the Vandals, ancient German people, invaded Rome by sea, looting the city of its treasury and enslaving its citizens. Prior to the Vandals' invasion, the Visigoths (Western Goths) under their leader Alaric in 410 fought Rome to a victorious conclusion in the Battle of Adrianople. Imperial Rome's demise was just a matter of time.

The events that led up to the fall of Imperial Rome can be traced to several factors. First, agriculture declined as farmers found it unprofitable to plant, flocking instead to the cities, where they became wards of the state. Second, heavy taxes to support wars left citizens with less to spend, causing businesses to fold; hence, prosperity declined. Third, jobless men could no longer afford matrimony, and this factor, coupled with a high abortion rate, resulted in a falling birth rate. Also, political disinterest on the part of the citizenry led to poor leadership. The moral fabric of the society began to tear apart as degenerating spectacles in the arena occupied the minds of the unemployed masses. Finally, Rome became dependent on foreigners, often subjugated peoples, to defend its borders and to fight its wars as fewer Romans were available for conscription. Foreigners obviously had no true ties to the motherland. Rome had been founded in 753 B.C. Caesar Augustus was its greatest emperor, from 27 B.C to A.D. 14 giving the empire the Pax Romana, or Roman Peace.

HADRIAN II

Last Married Pope: Pope Hadrian II, who led the Roman Catholic Church from December 14, 867, to December 872, was the last married pope. He succeeded Pope Nicholas I, the Great.

PAPAL RESIDENCE

Last Papal Residence Outside Italy: From 1309 until January 16, 1377, the Vatican was located at Avignon, France, because of political strife in Italy.

PLANTAGENET DYNASTY

Last of the Plantagenets: The ruling English dynasty was ended on September 30, 1399, with the abdication of King Richard II after he was imprisoned in the Tower of London. He was murdered on February 17, 1400.

Background: Having ruled in England since 1154, the Plantagenets, also called Angevins, were founded by Geoffrey, Count of Anjou. The name Plantagenet comes from the Latin *Planta genista,* which means broom, and Geoffrey actually wore a twig in his hat. Other Plantagenets include Henry II, Richard I, John Lackland, Henry III, Edward I, Edward II, and Edward III. The Plantagenets were succeeded by two warring houses— York and Lancaster.

BYZANTINE EMPIRE

Last Day: On May 29, 1453, just before dawn, the Turks, under the command of Sultan Mohammed II, razed the Byzantine capital Constantinople. The siege that began on April 22 ended with the deaths of almost seven thousand Byzantine troops and their leader, Emperor Constantine XI Palaeologus.

Background: The Byzantine Empire was founded by Constantine the Great in 330, with the formal separation from the west taking place in 395. The Byzantine Empire was Christian in religion with Greek and Asian populations. With the fall of Rome, the Byzantine Empire increased in influence, its domain consisting of Greece, western Anatolia, and the Balkans. Byzantine architecture—a style composed of a marriage of Greco-Roman and Oriental elements—is renowned. The fall of Constantinople marked historically the end of the Middle Ages.

HUNDRED YEARS WAR

Last Day: On October 19, 1453 the Earl of Shrewsbury died and the French towns that rose up in support of England surrendered.

Background: An on-again, off-again series of skirmishes, the Hundred Years War was a long drawn-out affair which began in 1337, when France sent troops to aid Scotland in her conflict with England. The Hundred Years War was vital to the very existence of France, whose throne was being claimed by England's Edward III. Four great battles fueled the war, with England winning three of them—the battles of Crecy, Poitiers, and Agincourt.

However, at the Battle of Orleans, a curious figure emerged. Her name was Joan of Arc. Her standard depicted God the Father, with fleur-de-lis and the words "Jesus, Maria." The English believed that she was a witch. Joan, clad in armor and wielding an ancient sword, led the siege of Orleans which intimidated the English, who were extremely superstitious. A future Roman Catholic saint, Joan was later captured and burned at the stake in 1431. The Battle of Orleans turned the tide of the Hundred Years War in favor of France. France defeated England, driving the English from French soil, except for Calais. The power of the French monarchy prevailed.

WARS OF THE ROSES

Last Day: With the death of the last of the York kings, Richard III, at the Battle of Bosworth, England, on August 22, 1485, the Wars of the Roses were over.

Background: England's Wars of the Roses were fought between the royal houses of York, whose symbol was a white rose, and Lancaster, whose emblem was a red rose. They were rival claimants to the English throne. The Wars of the Roses were begun more than a quarter of a century before, on July 10, 1460, when at the Battle of Northampton the Yorkists took the deranged King Henry VI prisoner. The Wars of the Roses would see their final chapter played out at the Battle of Bosworth. Richard III, the deformed king—one shoulder was higher than the other—was ambushed and clubbed to death by King Henry Tudor's soldiers. After the death of Richard III, Henry VII wed Elizabeth (1486), eldest daughter of King Edward IV of England, thus uniting the houses of York and Lancaster.

CHRISTOPHER COLUMBUS

Last Voyage: The fourth and last voyage of Columbus began in 1502 on May 11, when he set out from Spain, in the service of Queen Isabella, on four ships with a crew of 150, headed for the New World.

Background: The voyage took more than eight months in what was a difficult crossing with storms and declining provisions. The men had to resort to eating rats aboard ship that they could snare, shark meat, and dried wormy biscuits. The voyage was to bear some fruit for the explorer, among these the discovery of St. Lucia, Honduras, Costa Rica, and Panama.

Columbus returned to Spain on November 7, 1504, shortly before the death of his patron, Queen Isabella, on November 24. She had financed his four voyages to the New World. The fourth and last voyage was not considered a success, as among other trials, Columbus was marooned on the island of Jamaica for almost a year. Instead of returning to Spain with gold, as had been expected, the explorer brought back bananas, tobacco, palm oil, some coconuts, rabbits, and lizards.

Last Day of Life: Christopher Columbus died on May 20, 1506.

Background: The causes of Christopher Columbus's death cannot be traced for certain, but in the final days of his life he suffered from arthritis and swollen legs, and it is believed he had serious heart ailments. In any event, the final day of the explorer's life found him at Valladolid, a province in northwest Spain. The date was May 20, 1506. Having received the last rites of the Roman Catholic Church, he was barely able to take Holy Communion. Shortly after, his bed surrounded by friends and clergy, the great explorer passed away. He was fifty-five years old. To the last days of his life, Columbus believed that he had discovered an outlying part of Asia.

Born in Genoa, Italy, in 1451 (though that year is uncertain), Christopher Columbus was the greatest navigator of his time. At age ten, Columbus first went to sea, and he thereafter acquired a lifelong love of sea life. On one adventure, the young Columbus had his ship overtaken by pirates off the coast of Portugal. He later became a ship's captain. Unlike most contemporary sailors, Columbus believed the world was round. Columbus had an incurable ambition to find a westward route to the Indies. He first sought financing for his exploration from King John of Portugal, who refused him. Columbus then went to Queen Isabella of Spain. She agreed to underwrite the awesome voyage. Journeying on three ships, the *Nina, Pinta* and *Santa Maria,* sailing westward with 140 men, the explorer sighted the Bahamas, specifically an island that Columbus named San Salvador, on October 12, 1492. It was the first known European landing in the Americas since the eleventh century.

All the while Columbus believed he was in India. Three more voyages from Spain followed, the second in 1493, the third in 1498, and the last in 1502, voyages in which South America and Central America were discovered. Columbus's discoveries led to further European exploration and colonization in the New World and changed the course of history by proving that the world was indeed round.

ATAHUALPA

Last Inca of Peru: The Incan ruler Atahualpa was executed by strangulation on August 29, 1533, by the conquistadors led by Francisco Pizarro after being accused of plotting against the Spaniards. The passing of Peru's last Inca ended the Incan Dynasty begun in 1438 by the Inca Pachacutec.

Background: A ransom of gold, silver, gems, and valuable marble artifacts was demanded by the Spaniard Pizarro for the release of Peru's last Inca (the title for emperor). But the Spanish broke their promise. Spanish rule in

Peru lasted for almost three centuries from 1531 until November 9, 1824, when over nine thousand Spanish soldiers lost their lives to a Peruvian force of five thousand troops in the Battle of Ayacucho. Though Peru declared her independence in 1821, it took the Battle of Ayachucho to achieve its goal of complete freedom. Today Peru is a republic with a president and a premier.

HENRY VIII

Last Marriage: King Henry VIII of England took Catherine Parr as wife number six on July 12, 1543.

Background: Catherine Parr survived the cruel and inconsistent Henry by taking kindly care of her husband the last three years of his life, until he died on January 28, 1547. Parr carried on as queen dowager, caring for Henry's children, Edward VI, Mary I, and Elizabeth I. Other wives of Henry VIII: Catherine of Aragon (1485–1536), divorced; Anne Boleyn (1507–1536), executed after being charged with adultery; Jane Seymour (1509–1537), died giving birth; Anne of Cleves (1515–1557), lost Henry when marriage was declared invalid; and Catherine Howard (1521–1542), executed after being charged with adultery.

Last Day of Life: The corpulent English king died on January 28, 1547.

Background: Henry VIII fell victim to his vices. Famous for his large appetite, Henry weighed over four hundred pounds and his legs were a mass of ulcers. Servants had to lift him from one place to another, for he could hardly walk. He suffered from dropsy as a result of syphilis and from cirrhosis of the liver. Having gone into a coma at his palace at Whitehall in London, on January 27, 1547, Henry VIII died the following morning. Born at the royal palace in Greenwich near London on June 28, 1491, he was fifty-six years old.

Henry VIII of the House of Tudor began his reign in 1505 as a good and responsible king. But he was a man of great passion; a lover of fine food, beautiful women, and power. The Roman Catholic Church, which played a vital part in English life, was also important to Henry, as most of his countrymen were Catholic. Henry once even earned the title Defender of the Faith. Henry had personally commanded English forces against France to victory at the Battle of Spurs (1513); a month later, his troops defeated and killed James IV of Scotland at Flodden.

Unfortunately, the world knows Henry VIII as an overbearing king who executed several of his wives and his own advisers and ministers, including Thomas More, mostly because they would not secure his annulment from one spouse so that he might take another. In his dispute with Rome, Henry obtained from Parliament the Act of Supremacy in 1534, which created a national church, the Church of England, separate from the Roman Catholic Church. Henry became sole head of the church and its clergy; he also confiscated Roman Catholic Church property and closed monasteries. His wives one by one either died giving birth or fell victim to his madness.

IVAN THE TERRIBLE

Last Day of Life: Ivan the Terrible, the first czar of Russia, died on March 18, 1584.

Background: Ivan the Terrible was a very sick man, suffering from severe syphilis and mental illness. On the last day of his life, March 18, 1584, Ivan was happy after responding to his daily medication, given by a team of attending physicians. At his Kremlin suite, Ivan completed a refreshing bath and called for a chess board. Fumbling with the chess pieces as he sang Russian songs, Ivan began to gasp for breath and collapsed backward, landing on a bed. His face turned blue from lack of oxygen. Ivan the Terrible died before aid could be administered, at age fifty-four.

Ivan the Terrible was the first Russian monarch to formally assume the title czar (meaning Caesar). His crowning took place at age sixteen in 1547, and he was officially known as Ivan IV, Czar of Muscovy. Ivan IV had dreams of conquest as he sought to expand Russian territory. With a brutality and savagery that would earn him the name Terrible, Ivan IV massacred the Tatars at Kazan and Astrakhan in eastern Russia in 1552, gaining for Russia the mighty Volga River.

Only his gentle and loving wife, Anastasia Zakharina-Koshkins, had some salutary influence on her husband, but not enough to control his passion for spilling blood. Her death on August 7, 1560, left Ivan a desolate man. A decade after his wife's death, his vilest atrocities were committed against the people of the Russian city of Great Novgorod. A rumor had spread that some of the citizens of Great Novgorod were in sympathy with Poland in the Poland-Sweden-Russian Livonian War (1557–1582), a conflict over disputed territories. Great Novgorod was a prosperous city with a rich cultural life. Carefully closing off the city from the outside world for five weeks beginning in January 1570, he had hundreds of people murdered with unspeakable savagery. No form of torture was too heinous to satisfy the mad czar. Children, women, old people, and the clergy were mutilated. Farm goods, gold, silver, family possessions—anything of value—were carried away by Ivan's soldiers. No structure of the city was left with a roof, while animals, cattle, chickens, and even dogs were destroyed. Hundreds of citizens perished from starvation and the freezing temperatures. When the czar pulled out of Novgorod on February 15, 1570, the city was left lifeless.

But fate made the czar a victim of his own passions— one of these being rage. Afflicted with such a fit of anger, Ivan killed his son, leaving himself with unconsolable grief. The death of his son meant that the czar would be succeeded by another son, Fedor, who was mentally retarded.

TUDOR DYNASTY

Last Day: On March 24, 1603, with the death of Elizabeth I at age sixty-nine, the Tudor Dynasty was ended.

Background: The Tudor Dynasty was a house of high culture. The Tudor period was characterized by the four-

poster bed and elaborate oak furniture. The house of
English kings was founded by Owen Tudor, of an old
Welsh family, and its first king was Henry VII in 1485,
grandson of Owen Tudor. The dynasty lasted 118 years.
Also of the Tudor House were Henry VIII, Edward VI,
and Mary I. Mary I was also called Bloody Mary, as she
instigated religious persecution resulting in the deaths
of 280 persons, including the Protestant Archbishop of
Canterbury, Thomas Cranmer. The Tudors were succeeded by the Stuart Dynasty.

JAMES VI

Last Monarch of Independent Scotland: The last monarch
of independent Scotland was King James VI. In 1603
James VI succeeded to the throne of England upon the
death of Queen Elizabeth I on March 24 and took the
new title King James I. With James as king, Scotland and
England were united.

THIRTY YEARS WAR

Last Day: The Peace of Westphalia ended the Thirty Years
War on October 24, 1648.

Background: Begun in May 1618, the Thirty Years War,
a religious war, embroiled Sweden, France, Denmark,
and England against the mighty Hapsburgs who represented the Holy Roman Empire. The war, which the
Hapsburgs justified in an attempt to gain control of the
German states, broke out in Bohemia when Protestants
threw two Catholic administrators from a window at the
outbreak of a revolt. The Bohemians proceeded to overthrow their king, Ferdinand, and march on Austria with
mercenary soldiers. The war spread to Bavaria, then to
Denmark, Sweden, and finally France. England had sent
troops and funds to Denmark when that nation entered
the war. When the war ended thirty years later, Germany
had lost almost half her population, with nearly all her
cities destroyed. The Hapsburgs had failed to gain control of the German states, while France gained the re-

gion of Alsace. The Holy Roman Empire had begun to decline. The Thirty Years War was the last of the great wars the world would see until World War I. Ironically, the biggest loser of the Thirty Years War was Germany, who would suffer the same fate in the next two international wars—World War I and World War II.

WAR OF THE SPANISH SUCCESSION

Last Day: On April 11, 1712, the Treaty of Utrecht ended the war of the Spanish Succession.

Background: The king of Spain, Carlos II (1661–1700), was dying. His heir would soon combine the nations of Spain and France into one mighty kingdom. Fearing that this great state would dominate everyone, England and many other European states engaged in battle. This large, international conflict was the first time that nations considered what is today called the balance of power in Europe. The War of the Spanish Succession involved almost all the ruling houses of Europe. In North America the war was called Queen Anne's War. In the end, Louis XIV's grandson (Philip of Anjou) agreed to rule only Spain as Philip V. Louis XIV of France made several concessions, among them giving up territories in North America and recognizing Great Britain's Protestant succession.

LOUIS XIV

Last Day of Life: King Louis XIV of France died at Versailles on September 1, 1715.

Background: France's Louis XIV suffered from the ills of old age, with poor circulation and some feebleness, and when his leg became infected with gangrene, it spelled the end. On September 1, 1715, at the Palace of Versailles, having taken the necessary steps for a successful transition of power to his heir, the Duke of Anjou, and having received the last rites of the Roman Catholic Church, Louis said his last words, "Now and at the hour of my death, help me, oh God." Louis expired shortly after dawn. Born September 5, 1638 at St. Germain-en-laye, France, he was seventy-six years old.

Known as the Sun King, Louis XIV of France, the man who proclaimed "I am the state," had two sides to his reign. On the one hand, he took France to its height of commercial prosperity, which included the building of the mighty and sumptuous Palace of Versailles with its Hall of Mirrors. Louis XIV's reign lasted seventy-two years, which took France to the zenith of culture, a golden age of arts and letters.

But the other side of Louis XIV's reign was quite dark, for the poor became poorer, while the army under his power grew stronger and thus allowed Louis to embark on a series of conquests for new territories. Such conquests included struggles with Spain and parts of the Netherlands as well as Luxembourg—conflicts that paled in comparison to what was to come: the War of the Spanish Succession, which cost France in territory and prestige, and, worse, created a huge debt and greater poverty and desperation for the French people.

Another mistake of Louis was his persecution of the Protestant Huguenots. As Louis used his monarchical authority as a despotic tool, he could not foresee that upon his death the seeds of revolution would yield a bitter harvest in 1789 with the beginning of the French Revolution.

SEVEN YEARS WAR

Last Day: February 10, 1763, marked the conclusion of the Seven Years War.

Background: The Seven Years War began when Frederick the Great of Prussia (a former kingdom of North Europe, dissolved in 1947) invaded Saxony in 1756 because Empress Maria Theresa of the Holy Roman Empire had formed a coalition with Russia, Sweden, France, and Saxony. Empress Maria Theresa wanted Silesia, which she had lost in the War of Austrian Succession (1740–1748). Great Britain came in on the side of Prussia. Both France and Great Britain were already involved in a quest for colonization of the New World.

Prussia might have lost the Seven Years War but for the death of Elizabeth of Russia, which resulted in the ascendancy of Peter III to the Russian throne. Peter III (married to Catherine the Great), friendly with Frederick, reconciled with Prussia and became her ally. In the end, Empress Maria Theresa, without Russia as an ally, was forced to come to terms with the Peace of Paris. Prussia and Great Britain were the victors, but not without a price. Prussia lost almost a million of her people—soldiers and civilians—to this war.

AMERICAN REVOLUTION

Last Official Day: The official last day of the American Revolution was May 12, 1784, when the peace treaties were exchanged between the two nations.

Background: The Continental Congress had formally announced an end to all hostilities against Great Britain on April 17, 1783, and the United States had ratified the Treaty of Paris on January 14, 1784. The United States negotiators included Benjamin Franklin, John Adams, John Jay, and Henry Laurnes. Negotiating for Great Britain was Richard Oswald.

The essential provisions of the Treaty of Paris called for Great Britain to recognize the sovereignty and independence of the United States. All hostilities were to end, with Great Britain withdrawing from U.S. territories. U.S. fishing rights and boundaries were to be officially recognized as well.

The American Revolution for independence from Great Britain pitted American colonists against the British government. The war spanned some twenty years, from 1763 to 1783. The thirteen colonies revolted against British dominance, specifically the way they were taxed without any voice in the process. The Boston Tea Party, a protest against a new British tax on tea in which colonists dumped a cargo of tea into Boston Harbor, was one of the boldest moves toward all-out war.

In 1775 the Continental Congress appointed George Washington commander-in-chief of the Continental

Army. The Battle of Bunker Hill on January 17, 1775, was the first significant battle of the war. Some 250 British soldiers were killed, with another thousand soldiers wounded. The Continental Army lost 140 men with almost five thousand soldiers wounded. On July 4, 1776, the Continental Congress adopted the Declaration of Independence from Great Britain (celebrated by Americans annually on July 4, Independence Day). The Declaration of Independence absolved the colonists of their allegiance to the British crown. On June 14, 1777, the Continental Congress adopted its new flag, consisting of alternating red and white stripes with thirteen stars—one star to represent each of the thirteen colonies.

By the end of the year, on December 17, 1777, France, a decade before her own revolution, recognized the legitimacy of the Union of Colonies to exist independent of Great Britain. Such victories as the Battle of Trenton, on December 26, 1776, after George Washington's famous crossing of the Delaware River that surprised the Hessians, inspired the Americans to even more victories. On December 19, 1782, the Continental Army scored a decisive victory over the British redcoats and General Charles O'Hara handed over his sword in surrender to General Benjamin Lincoln of the Continental Army at Yorktown. Eight thousand British soldiers were taken prisoners, and the war was over. But a final battle occurred on March 10, 1783, at sea. The U.S. ship *Alliance* turned back the British *Sybil*, after which the *Sybil* suddenly silenced her guns and sailed away.

A new nation was born—the United States of America—and by its two hundredth birthday, the nation, a true democracy, would consist of fifty states, one of the most powerful nations on earth.

RHODE ISLAND

Last State to Ratify the Constitution: Rhode Island, on May 29, 1790, accepted the United States Constitution. Delaware had been the first state to ratify.

LOUIS XVI

Last Day of Life: King Louis XVI of France was beheaded on January 21, 1793.

Background: On Monday, January 21, 1793, Louis XVI was awakened just after 5 in the morning, feeling well rested. The National Convention—the revolutionary court—had found the king guilty of conspiracy against French liberty on January 17.

He showed no fear or anxiety over his impending fate. Dressed by his valet Clery, Louis knelt for a private Mass said in his cell, a small suite of rooms in a medieval fortress of the old Templar knights called the Temple, in Paris. To have the priest say Mass was a concession accorded the king, for the Roman Catholic priest, Henry Essex Edgeworth de Firmont, had not taken the oath of allegiance to the republic. Receiving Communion, the king was afterward given a last blessing. At peace, Louis confided to Edgeworth, "How happy I am to have my principles. Where would I be without them. With them, even death appears sweet to me. Yes, there exists an incorruptible judge in heaven who will know how to give me the justice that men refuse me here."

At 9 o'clock the commander of the national guard arrived for the king and the long ride to the scaffold. Louis had taken no breakfast. The January morning was typically wintry, damp and foggy for Paris. Soldiers lined the way to the guillotine, a quiet and behaved crowd behind them. Louis, in an enclosed coach was absorbed in his prayers from the Abbe de Firmont's breviary. At the site of execution, the drums sounded their steady tattoo. Louis's hair had recently been cut, and he stood coatless as the drums stopped. "I die innocent," the king said. "I pardon my enemies and I hope that my blood will be useful to the French, that it will appease God's anger . . . " The surge of the drums on orders from the commander drowned out the king as he continued to speak. Louis's neck was fitted into execution position. In the brief time left to him, the king cried out his last words, "May my blood cement the happiness of

Fra—'' The guillotine's knife had crashed, beheading the king. A roar went up from the crowd. Louis XVI, born in 1754, was thirty-eight years old.

MARIE ANTOINETTE

Last Day of Life: The queen of France died on October 16, 1793, some nine months after her husband's execution.

Background: Marie Antoinette spent most of the night and the dawn of her last hours composing a farewell letter to her sister, until her maid entered her chilly cell at 7 o'clock in the morning and observed the queen to be almost disfigured from weariness and menstrual hemorrhaging. Declining to take breakfast (usually chocolate, coffee, some fruit, and dairy products), the queen only wished the final comfort of going to the scaffold with dignity. She put on clean garments with the help of her sympathetic maid, who tidied up the cell. The queen, undergoing her monthly travail, took special care to conceal her blood-soiled chemise in a crevice behind the stove in her cell, knowing that after she departed the premises, prying eyes would scrutinize anything left behind.

Refusing to make a final confession of sins to a priest who had taken the oath of loyalty to the Republic of France, the queen prayed silently, while outside her cell beyond the Conciergerie—a massive stone prison—thousands of armed soldiers stood nervously to thwart any attempt that might be made to save the queen.

At 10 o'clock that morning the executioner, Sanson, arrived to prepare the queen for death. Bravely Marie Antoinette submitted to having her hands tied behind her back. Dressed in a white gown and new plum-colored shoes, her prematurely gray hair covered by a two-winged cap, the queen was helped into a wagon and seated backward for the ride to the scaffold. Amid the throngs, the once-beautiful queen was hardly recognized. Her beauty was gone, replaced by gaunt features, and eyes that were youthful yet old. She had had months to ponder the strange series of events that had turned all France against her. On her dress close to her heart was a scapular of the Sacred Heart of Jesus. The crowd was silent, the sky hazy. This woman about to die had once been a careless child who wanted love more than power; what could she understand at fourteen, when her mother, the great Maria Theresa, informed her that she had just signed her marriage contract. No doubt the powerful leader of Austria told the starry-eyed child that the alliance the marriage would bring would be most advantageous to Austria. Like all young women hopeful of a handsome suitor, perhaps she inquired about the physical stature of her future husband, and might have asked, Is he nice?

Only two days before her trip to the guillotine the queen had been found guilty of inciting war with foreign nations. With Louis gone, her children taken from her, death might not have seemed so unbearable. As she mounted the platform, her last words were an apology to the executioner for having mistakenly stepped on his feet: "Monsieur, I beg your pardon. I did not do it on purpose." Standing on the platform, Marie Antoinette discerned the revolutionary leaders Robespierre and Danton in the crowd. The queen was thrust ungently by Sanson and forced to kneel. Her head was placed through the "widow's window" of the guillotine. A clanging chain sound from the death machine was heard, the knife was set in motion, and Marie Antoinette was gone. Her life spanned the years 1755–1793; she was thirty-seven years old.

CATHERINE THE GREAT

Last Day of Life: Catherine the Great, Empress of Russia, died on November 17, 1796.

Background: At the time of her death, Catherine the Great was quite feeble and overweight. In her prime, she had been tall, statuesque and very beautiful. At her palace at St. Petersburg, Russia on November 5, 1796, Catherine the Great suffered the first of two strokes while in her private chambers. A second stroke followed shortly after and proved to be fatal, leaving her lingering near death until she expired on November 17, 1796. She was sixty-seven years old.

Catherine the Great, formerly Princess Sophie Fredericke Augusta of Anhalt, came into prominence with her marriage to Peter III of Russia in 1744. After Peter was murdered by Catherine's lover, she was proclaimed empress of all Russia in 1762. To survive as a foreigner among the nobles of Russia, Catherine granted them freedom from taxes and military service, for she in truth had no legal right to the throne.

Once having firmly established her power, Catherine the Great showed signs of autocratic and arbitrary leadership, favoring nobles over the poor. The empress transferred state lands to the nobility, which increased serfdom, most notably in the Ukraine. Catherine proved to be an expansionist, increasing Russian dominance over Poland by installing her relative on the Polish throne. She went to war against Turkey, which weakened the Ottoman Empire when some of its domains fell into Russian hands. In 1783 Catherine added the Crimea to Russian territory after it had gained its independence from Turkey. Though a patron of the arts and letters, Catherine the Great did not rule with integrity, favoring aristocrats over the poor, a practice that continued long after her death through the reign of the czars and only ended with the Russian Revolution of 1917.

GEORGE WASHINGTON
(First President of the United States)

Last Day in Office: March 4, 1797, after two terms.

Background: Married to wealthy widow Martha Custis, who had four children, George Washington did not have children of his own. He coined the phrase "Mr. President," bowed when introduced to people, allowed no swearing in his presence, wore a white wig over red-brown hair, and had several pairs of false teeth made not of wood, but of hippopotamus ivory filled with pure gold. He so loved his horses, he saw to it that their teeth were brushed. At his death, he was worth more than a half million dollars.

CASANOVA

Last Romance: Casanova's last love affair was one pursued by correspondence with Cecile Roggensdorff of Dresden, Germany, in 1797, when the Italian adventurer was seventy-two years old.

Background: In the last months of his life, Casanova, the world's greatest lover, was employed as a librarian in Bohemia at Count Waldstein's castle at Dux, working on his memoirs. He began writing love letters to the beautiful Cecile Roggensdorff. It was Casanova's last romantic adventure and came about when a certain noble, Count Roggensdorff, his fortune gone, wrote to Casanova begging him to use his influence to recommend his fair sister for some high position. Cecile, upon being enlightened about her brother's audacious behavior, wrote to Casanova begging his pardon. Many letters followed, with Cecile and Casanova declaring their love for each other. Casanova promised to will his fifteen volumes of memoirs to her, and through Casanova's influence, Cecile Roggensdorff was able to acquire a position as lady-in-waiting at the court of a famous duke. Casanova and Cecile were destined never to see each other, for death came to the world's most famous romantic on June 4, 1798, when he died peacefully at age seventy-three, less than a year after he and Cecile first became acquainted. He was born Giovanni Jacopo in Venice, Italy, on April 2, 1725.

FRENCH REVOLUTION

Last Day: On December 14, 1799, Napoleon Bonaparte was declared First Consul of France, thus abolishing the Directory that was formed in 1795, more than a year after the Reign of Terror.

Background: The French Revolution began in 1789 and spanned a decade, with its bloodiest period lasting from

1791 until the death of Robespierre in 1794. On June 20, 1789, a group of French lawyers and nobles, all of the poor third estate class, met on a tennis court after Louis XVI forbade them to meet in their own hall. On the court, which was located in one of the buildings under the palace, they took an oath—since called the Tennis Court Oath, and, calling themselves the National Assembly, vowed to draw up a French constitution. With the French lower classes, or third estate, suffering under the weight of crushing taxes and soaring wheat prices, rumors began to surface that the aristocracy in league with the king were planning to starve the people.

On July 14, 1789, a huge mob of citizens stormed the notorious Bastille. The Bastille, a prison said to house political prisoners, was destroyed when the inmates, many murderers among them, were set free. In October 1789 a mob of ragged women and children besieged the Palace of Versailles, breaking windows with picks and shovels. Queen Marie Antoinette escaped from the bloodthirsty mob through a back entrance. Within a year most of France was in turmoil. Churches, monasteries, and many of the wealthy estates and lands had been closed and confiscated for sale to the poor. New money, called assignate, which had been issued under the ruling National Assembly, had bankrupted the nation, making gold and silver the only trading currency. The clergy, largely Catholic, were not allowed to practice their faith unless they took an oath of allegiance to the Assembly.

By early 1792 three figures emerged—Maximilien Robespierre, Jean Marat, and George Danton—each prominent in the years called the Reign of Terror. On March 25, 1792, the National Assembly officially adopted the guillotine as the state means of dispensing death. From daybreak to late afternoon, day after day, thousands viewed the tumbrels with the unfortunate souls, women and children among them, to be beheaded. On September 21, 1792, the monarchy was abolished, and on January 21, 1793, Louis XVI was guillotined; his queen, Marie Antoinette, followed him to her death on October 16, 1793.

By the time the Reign of Terror was over, more than seventeen thousand people had died on the guillotine. Near the close of the Reign of Terror, trials were held with juries passing death sentences without hearing evidence or arguments. The Reign of Terror ended July 29, 1794, with the death of Robespierre. Yet another wave of violence followed as France sought to apprehend those associated with Robespierre. A year after the death of Robespierre the French government established the Directory, but it was corrupt. The country languished in terrible privation, with the army in control and the guillotine still beheading former terrorists from the bloody days of revolution. It took a young soldier, Napoleon Bonaparte—to some a saint, to others a scoundrel—to put France on a stable course. Napoleon once said of his good fortune, "I found the crown of France lying on the ground and I picked it up with a sword!"

GEORGE WASHINGTON
(First President of the United States)

Last Day of Life: George Washington died on December 14, 1799.

Background: On December 13, 1799, despite feeling unwell due to exposure to fierce wintry weather the previous day, America's first president rode his steed through the snows of his Mount Vernon, Virginia, fields. It was very cold but he went out surveying trees to be felled, oblivious to a painful sore throat. That night he slept poorly and would not let his concerned wife, Martha, seek help. On December 14, his doctor arrived, gave him a laxative medicine, took blood, and applied poultices. The former president could hardly breathe and felt himself sinking. His doctor decided to make a tiny incision in his throat, but then his breathing improved. By late evening Washington gave instructions on how he wished to be buried. Fearful of being buried while still alive, he ordered that he not be buried until two days after he was presumed to be dead. Just before 10 o'clock at night, George Washington touched his own wrist to feel a pulse; with a fading glance at his wife and his doctor, he spoke his last words: "I thank you for your attention. You had better not take any more trouble about me, but let me go off quietly. I cannot last long." Having spoken these words, Washington passed away. Born on February 22, 1732, in Virginia, he was sixty-seven years old.

Gravesite: Mount Vernon, Virginia.

JOHN ADAMS
(Second President of the United States)

Last Day in Office: March 4, 1801, after one term.

Background: Reputed to have been arrogant and obnoxious, John Adams was also one of the most honest of men, and staunchly patriotic. His wife was Abigail Adams, and like her husband, she was outspoken. Their marriage lasted fifty-four years. His signature is on the Declaration of Independence, and the day of his death marks the fifty-year anniversary of his signing. His son, John Quincy Adams, served as President also, the only time in history that a father and son have both been president of the United States.

HOLY ROMAN EMPIRE

Last Day: When Napoleon bound the German states to himself by the Confederation of the Rhine on July 12, 1806, the Holy Roman Empire ended. Exempt were Austria and Russia.

Background: The Holy Roman Empire began more than a thousand years before on Christmas Day in the year 800, when Charlemagne was crowned emperor by Pope Leo III, giving him rule over all the German-speaking lands. Though Charlemagne had the Church's blessing, he in fact regarded himself as the leader of the Church. Charlemagne's true ideal was a theocracy similar to that of ancient Palestine when King Solomon ruled. The Holy Roman Empire gave rise to four major dynasties, the Saxon Dynasty (936–1024), the Salian or Franconian Dynasty (1024–1125), the Hohenstaufen Dynasty and rivals (1238–1256) and the mighty Hapsburg House, beginning with Emperor Rudolph I in 1273 to the last ruler of the Holy Roman Empire, Francis II, who went on to become emperor of Austria. The Holy Roman Empire was also regarded as the first German Reich.

THOMAS JEFFERSON
(Third President of the United States)

Last Day in Office: March 4, 1809, after two terms.

Background: Thomas Jefferson was an author, architect, inventor (he invented the dumb waiter and a copying machine), and musician (violinist), and he was also tall, fair, and handsome. He had a way with language that raised spirits as well as tempers: "Every difference of opinion is not a difference of principle." "A little rebellion now and then is a good thing, and as necessary in the political world as storms in the physical."

WAR OF 1812

Last Day: June 30, 1815, marked the end of the war of 1812.

Background: The war was begun on June 18, 1812, between the United States and Great Britain over freedom of the seas. The United States prevailed, though the war continued for more than six months after the Treaty of Ghent (signed on Christmas Eve, 1814, officially ending the conflict), because of a poorly drawn treaty and a lack of communication. The War of 1812 is remembered for James Lawrence's last words: "Don't give up the ship! Sink it, blow it up." Lawrence was in command of the ship *Chesapeake,* which, after a fierce battle, lost to the British frigate *Shannon.* "The Chesapeake" was towed off by the British to Halifax. During the War of 1812 Francis Scott Key wrote an anthem entitled "The Defense of Fort McHenry," later retitled "The Star-Spangled Banner."

JAMES MADISON
(Fourth President of the United States)

Last Day in Office: March 4, 1817, after two terms.

Background: The last surviving signer of the U.S. Constitution, James Madison was known for his retiring manner. He was not very tall, and he did not marry until age forty-three. His wife, the former Dolley Todd, a widow, was quite beautiful and an extrovert who as Dolley Madison enhanced her husband's presidency through her social graces. Madison understood the importance of the Union of the new nation, and whether dealing with the Federalists or the Indians, both of whom he disliked, peace and compromise were important to him. He had cooperated with John Jay and Alexander Hamilton in writing the Federalist Papers, essays that explained the U.S. Constitution and its practical implementations. Madison sought the friendship of the Indians by inviting a large group to the White House for friendly meetings.

NAPOLEON BONAPARTE

Last Day of Life: Emperor Napoleon Bonaparte of France died on May 5, 1821.

Background: Having suffered from tuberculosis for the greater part of his life, the French leader contracted hepatitis while on the island of St. Helena, the place of his exile. Other health conditions included a problem with his weight and discomfort from malaria and hearing loss. Yet Napoleon's energies did not wane as he hurried to put his papers in order. However, on March 22, 1821, the French leader succumbed to vomiting spells and began to bleed internally. Given some medicine intended to work as a laxative, Napoleon contracted a severe case of diarrhea with increased bleeding. On May 5, at 5:49 P.M., he said his last words:

"God! . . . France! . . .My son! . . . Josephine!" The end came, with Napoleon's eyes still open but lifeless. Cause of death was cancer of the stomach. Born on August 15, 1769, at Ajaccio Corsica, France, he was fifty-one years old.

Napoleon I, considered one of the greatest conquerors who ever lived, after college was trained at military schools for a career in the French army. He first gained military prominence in 1795 with his defense of the Paris gardens known as the Tuileries. From then on, with his promotion to commander of the Army Interior at age twenty-six, he embarked on a series of vital conquests, among them the Italian and Egyptian campaigns (1796–1804). Napoleon's Italian campaign—including a treacherous crossing of the Alps and St. Bernard Pass—was most successful with a victory at Lodi and the conquering of Northern Italy for France.

His quest for Egypt was a disaster, however. Crowned emperor in 1804, Napoleon waged a series of wars known as the Napoleonic Wars, which began in 1805 after he crowned himself king of Italy. Napoleon created a nobility and a court that included installing rulers in Spain, Holland, Italy, and Sweden. These acts only increased the resolve of countries such as Great Britain, already at war with Napoleon, to defeat him.

His invasion of Russia in 1808 was very costly in manpower. It failed because of the harsh weather and the fact that the Russian people had burned their city rather than turn its goods and supplies over to Napoleon. The Battle of Leipzig in 1813 was also unfortunate for Napoleon as it cost him both Germany and Poland. Confidence in Napoleon fell as his former allies turned against him, and in 1814 Napoleon abdicated.

Exiled to the island of Elba, the French leader returned to France in 1815 to begin his famous One Hundred Days, a time spent in attempting to regain past glory by reestablishing his empire. Napoleon failed with his stunning defeat at Waterloo at the hands of Wellington and the British in 1815. Having abdicated for a second time, Napoleon surrendered and was exiled to the island of St. Helena in the south Atlantic, where he died.

The opinions of historians are divided on this great leader who took France from the crises of the French Revolution back to the road of stability. Some believe he was a power-hungry despot who exploited the French Revolution to his own ends; others see him as a savior, a great administrator, and a military genius.

JAMES MONROE
(Fifth President of the United States)

Last Day in Office: March 4, 1825, after two terms.

Background: Monroe was the last survivor of the Founding Fathers. His presidency is remembered for a document that bears his name, the Monroe Doctrine, which states that the United States will not interfere in European affairs and will not tolerate European interference in American affairs. Nothing more profound would mark James Monroe's presidency, called an Era of Good Feeling.

THOMAS JEFFERSON
(Third President of the United States)

Last Day of Life: Thomas Jefferson died on July 4, 1826.

Background: One of America's most gifted presidents retired to his estate, Monticello, southeast of Charlottesville, Virginia, aware that he was not well. The man who composed the words, "All men are created equal" in the Declaration of Independence was coming upon that day when those words would be most remembered—July 4, fifty years later, in 1826. With his family and servants at his bedside, Jefferson cooled his parched tongue with water from a sponge. Soon the dawn would be streaking across the eastern sky, and happy souls throughout America would be celebrating what is simply known as the Fourth. From Jefferson's lips came his last words: "Is it the Fourth? I resign my spirit to God, my daughter, to my country." Jefferson lingered near death throughout the morning, until at 1 o'clock in the afternoon, he expired. His death was due to ill health. Born in Virginia on April 13, 1743, he was eighty-three years old.

Gravesite: Monticello Memorial Park, Charlottesville, Virginia.

JOHN ADAMS
(Second President of the United States)

Last Day of Life: John Adams died on July 4, 1826.

Background: Various illnesses stalked America's second president, but he was ninety years of age and this was not unusual. Sciatica, excessive weight gain, and poor eyesight affected him, but he was also a highly excitable man. In the afternoon of July 4, 1826, as he sat in a thick cushioned chair, his vital signs gave little indication of life. His last words were: "Thomas Jefferson still survives." (Jefferson, by coincidence, had passed away earlier that very day). As twilight cooled the summer day, John Adams gave up his spirit. He was born on October 30, 1735, in Quincy, Massachusetts.

Gravesite: First Unitarian Church, Quincy, Massachusetts.

JOHN QUINCY ADAMS
(Sixth President of the United States)

Last Day in Office: March 4, 1829, after one term.

Background: The son of John Adams, second president of the United States, John Quincy Adams is remembered for his morning dips in the Potomac River and for favoring honesty over loyalty in his Cabinet choices. His presidency was uneventful, and four years after his election he lost the nation's top office to Andrew Jackson.

JAMES MONROE
(Fifth President of the United States)

Last Day of Life: James Monroe died on July 4, 1831.

Background: Having caught a cold, James Monroe came down with tuberculosis. On Independence Day, July 4, 1831, the fifth president of the United States died peacefully at 3 o'clock in the morning in New York City. Born on April 28, 1758 in Westmoreland, Virginia, he was seventy-three years old.

Gravesite: Hollywood Cemetery, Richmond, Virginia.

INQUISITION

Last Day: July 15, 1834.

Background: The Inquisition (Latin *inquirere,* "to look into"), was a period of inquiry, punishment, and prevention of heresy that began in southern France under Pope Gregory IX in 1229. Its purpose was to halt the spread of Albigensianism, a heretic sect that repudiated the Church sacraments, particularly marriage, while also opposing civil authority. These legal courts of the Inquisition were presided over by specially designated church officials to look into accusations of heresy, with the accused in most cases given the option of recanting in confirmation of their faith, with a small penance being meted out as punishment.

To understand the Inquisition, one must understand that in France, Belgium, Germany, and Spain—where the ecclesiastical-civil courts of inquiry were held, heresy according to the civil laws of the day was considered an act of treason and anarchy and was punishable by death. The ecclesiastical courts had jurisdiction only over Catholics, but the condemned were turned over to the civil authorities to face civil justice; these unfortunates often were subject to cruel punishment, which sometimes included burning at the stake. From the Church's point of view, the Inquisition was essentially concerned with instigating repentance and winning back errant Catholics. Abuses resulted when the state used the Inquisition as a means of political repression.

Perhaps the most famous figure (among many innocents who were persecuted) to be condemned by the

Inquisition was the Italian physicist and astronomer Galileo. In 1613, in his letters on the solar spots, Galileo advocated a theory of the Polish astronomer Copernicus that the earth revolved around the sun, while the Church held the belief that the sun revolved around the earth. The earth, according to the Church, was the central body of the universe. In a trial in 1615 Galileo was permitted to hold his scientific view as long as he did not defend it in public via publication. In 1632 the astronomer failed to observe the terms of his agreement with the Church by publishing his views and was taken before the Inquisition tribunal on April 12, 1633. Threatened with punishment on the rack if he did not retract his defense of Copernicus's system, Galileo surrendered and was allowed to retire for the rest of his life outside Florence, Italy.

The Inquisition, which had spread to Italy, then the Netherlands, eventually found its way to Spain, where the Spanish Inquisition (1478) exceeded Church bounds when civil courts used the Church as an excuse to terrorize, persecute, and murder. The Spanish Inquisition overshadowed what was begun as an ecclesiastical tool to abolish heresy. In the end, while the Inquisition did much to prevent the spread of Protestantism, in some countries, particularly the Netherlands, it sowed the seeds of permanent hatred for the Roman Catholic Church.

BATTLE OF THE ALAMO

Last Day: The Alamo fell to the Mexicans on March 6, 1836.

Background: On February 23, 1836, a battle began between Mexican regulars and 187 Texans who were seceding from Mexico for the purpose of setting up their own country. The Mexican forces were commanded by General Lopez de Santa Anna, and the Texans were under the command of Colonel William B. Travis. The small force of Texans held firm until the morning of March 6, costing Santa Anna huge military losses. Aware that too much blood had been shed, the Mexican general offered mercy if the Texans would surrender. Before the final siege of the fort, Travis sent a last message: "I shall never surrender or retreat—victory or death."

Mexican General Castrillon ordered cannon fire and a wave of soldiers to attack at sunrise. Cannon fire opened against the Mexicans, followed by an incessant hail of gunfire. Another wave of Mexican soldiers was ordered forth in the face of blazing rifles and small-arms fire. Among the defenders of the old adobe mission was Jim Bowie, famous for his knife expertise, and Davy Crockett, a Tenneseean. A third wave of soldiers had inflicted losses on the Texans at the walls. Cannon fire from within the fort had scattered the first mass of soldiers storming through the smoking walls. Fierce hand-to-hand combat ensued. The siege of the mission intensified as hundreds of Mexican soldiers charged the fort entrance. A furious blast of cannon fire from within the mission scored a direct hit on the massing troops, while torches ignited kegs of gunpowder. The last siege of soldiers met little resistance. The Alamo mission was surrounded, Bowie and Travis were slain, and the fort fell. A handful of prisoners, including Crockett, were stabbed to death by their Mexican captors after General Castrillon, directly responsible for the Mexican siege, brought the prisoners before Santa Anna.

The rallying cry "Remember the Alamo" became the inspiration for Texas independence. On April 21, a little over a month after the Alamo fell, Santa Anna's army was defeated by Texans under General Sam Houston at the Battle of San Jacinto. Following the victory, Texas declared her independence.

The Battle of the Alamo is named after the region, Alamo, which means cottonwood tree in Spanish, a tree native to the region.

JAMES MADISON
(Fourth President of the United States)

Last Day of Life: James Madison died on June 28, 1836.

Background: In Montpelier, Virginia, on June 28, 1836, the fourth president of the United States had trouble breathing and was unable to swallow some breakfast. Having spoken his last words: "I always talk better lying down," he did not speak again. At 6 o'clock in the morning, Madison stopped breathing, and an hour later he was pronounced dead. Born in Port Conway, Virginia, on March 16, 1751, he was eighty-five years old.

Gravesite: Montpelier Station, Virginia.

ANDREW JACKSON
(Seventh President of the United States)

Last Day in Office: March 4, 1837, after two terms.

Background: There never was a president like Andrew Jackson. He was noticeably unsmiling when he took his oath, for his rise to the presidency had been won at the expense of his wife, who had suffered emotionally from the harsh and critical campaign. The common man never had a stronger ally in the White House. Jackson mounted his horse for the procession to the White House and proceeded to ride right into his new home, where his friends, with their muddy boots and out doors-men-like manner, drank heartily, wolfed down the fare, pulled down the curtains, broke the furniture, carried away articles, and generally made nuisances of themselves. Many of the guests ended up sprawled drunk on the White House lawn.

The Jackson presidency was one of a fearless, even reckless, man in battle with the rich and powerful. Not afraid of confrontation, he was staunchly loyal to his friends. When his friend John Eaton married the beautiful Peggy O'Neale Timberlake, Jackson decided to reward Eaton by making him secretary of war. A scandal erupted when it was disclosed that the new Mrs. Eaton was a former innkeeper's daughter and had played a part in the suicide of one man and the questionable circumstances of the death of her first husband. Jackson stood by the Eatons and entreated the other wives of his Cabinet to treat her as one of the family. When the ladies refused, Jackson became enraged and kicked out the entire Cabinet.

But Jackson's most memorable act was his fight with the United States Bank—an institution that had been entrusted with over $10 million in government deposits. Its president, Nicholas Biddle, an arrogant aristocrat, despised Jackson for his commoner lineage. Without the charter under which it enjoyed large profits with the government deposits, the bank could not hope to survive. The bank's ally was Henry Clay, the presidential candidate whose campaign to unseat Jackson in his bid for a second term was supported with the bank's own funds. The bank seemed assured of winning and, in so doing, embarrassing Jackson, for Biddle felt the American people were behind him. But Jackson's "poor against the rich" speech persuaded the masses to vote for him. Jackson won, and the Bank of the United States was overthrown when the president vetoed its charter. Jackson then had the money deposited in state banks of his own choosing, called pet banks.

LIBERTY BELL

Last Day the Liberty Bell Rang: On July 8, 1838 the historic bell in Independence Hall, Philadelphia, cracked for the second and last time when it tolled in memory of Chief Justice John Marshall. It first rang officially on July 4, 1776, to declare American Independence.

MARTIN VAN BUREN

(Eighth President of the United States)

Last Day in Office: March 4, 1841, after one term.

Background: The eighth president of the United States was the first president who was born an American citizen. All previous holders of the office were once British subjects. The former vice president of the United States was remembered for his nicknames: Flying Dutchman, American Talleyrand, Little Magician, and Red Fox of Kinderhook. Soft-spoken, vain, a ladies' man, highly intelligent, and a skilled politician, he also had the misfortune of being hit by a bank scandal. Van Buren was absolved of any personal blame, but the scandal hurt his chances for reelection. He opposed the annexation of Texas, a hot issue of the day, and was against slavery.

WILLIAM HENRY HARRISON
(Ninth President of the United States)

Last Day of Life: William Henry Harrison died on April 4, 1841, having served thirty-two days of his first term as president.

Background: The ninth President of the United States wasn't afraid of the cold. On his Inauguration Day, his address to the nation took one hundred minutes; the last president born before the American Revolution made his address without coat, top hat, or even gloves, determined to show he was a vigorous sixty-eight years of age. (Before Ronald Reagan, who became president at age sixty-nine, Harrison was the oldest man to take the office.) For more than a month after, Harrison suffered a cold and sniffles; eventually, as he continued to ignore his condition, taking morning walks to the market to purchase his own meat and vegetables, his health finally gave out. On March 27 Harrison developed pneumonia. On the evening of April 4, he spoke his last words in delirium: "Sir, I wish you to understand the true principles of government. I wish them carried out. I ask nothing more," shortly before the fatal virus ended his life. He was born February 9, 1773, in Berkeley, Virginia.

Harrison had no political experience. Nominated by the Whigs, he used the slogan: "Tippecanoe and Tyler too" because Harrison was a war hero, having fought the Indians at the Battle of Tippecanoe in 1811; John Tyler was his vice president. Harrison had studied medicine but left medical school. In thirty-two days as president he became a permanent piece of American history.

Gravesite: Pioneer Cemetery, North Bend, Ohio.

JOHN TYLER
(Tenth President of the United States)

Last Day in Office: March 4, 1845. John Tyler became the tenth United States president upon the death of William Henry Harrison, who died while in office.

Background: America's tenth President had fifteen children, annexed Texas to the Union, and gave jobs to his relatives. His term was uneventful, though he did attract a lot of attention and caused much gossip when he married a woman twenty years his junior; it was his second marriage. Tyler gained his vice presidency via the Whig Party, then turned his back on the Whigs when he became chief executive, opposing their programs.

ANDREW JACKSON
(Seventh President of the United States)

Last Day of Life: Andrew Jackson died on June 8, 1845.

Background: Andrew Jackson suffered from consumption in his later years and always complained of aches and pains. He could not breathe without pain and was plagued with a chronic cough. His children were summoned to his bedside at his estate near Nashville, Tennessee, on June 8, 1845. Jackson requested his spectacles so that he might see his children for the last time. Observing tears in their eyes, Jackson asked, "What's the matter, my dear children? Have I alarmed you? Oh do not cry. Be good children, and we will all meet in heaven." At 6 o'clock that evening, less than an half hour after speaking with his children, Andrew Jackson passed away. Born March 15, 1767, in Waxhaw, South Carolina, he was seventy-eight years old.

Gravesite: The Hermitage, Old Hickory, Tennessee.

JOHN QUINCY ADAMS
(Sixth President of the United States)

Last Day of Life: John Quincy Adams died on February 23, 1848.

Background: On February 21, 1848, while at the House of Representatives in Washington, D.C., as John Quincy Adams was about to address his peers, he collapsed. He was taken to the Speakers Room to be cared for. With his wife and children at his side, he said his last words on February 23: "This is the last of earth. I am content." In the evening between 7:15 and 7:20, paralysis set in and he died at age eighty. He was born on July 11, 1767, in Birmington (now Quincy), Massachusetts. He was the last chief executive whose presidency was decided in the House of Representatives.

Gravesite: First Unitarian Church, Quincy, Massachusetts.

LOUIS PHILIPPE

Last Monarch of France: King Louis Philippe, the Citizen King, descendant of Louis XIII, reigned from 1830 until his abdication on February 24, 1848.

Background: King Louis Philippe succeeded Charles X, who had abdicated favoring his grandson, Comte de Chambord. But the French government had another choice and it was the king's lieutenant general, Duc d'Orleans, Louis Philippe. Louis Philippe was not responsive to the people; he became autocratic, while favoring close ties with England and winning few friends at home. Louis Philippe abdicated and France proclaimed its second republic on February 24, 1848. France had been ruled by kings since Hugh Capet in 987, with three houses reigning: the Capetians (987–1328), the House of Valois (1329–1589) and the House of Bourbon (1589–1792, temporarily suspended with the death of Louis XVI). The Bourbon House was restored with

Louis XVIII in 1814 and ended with Louis Philippe of the Bourbon-Orleans House. France is today in its fifth republic, with an elected president.

JAMES KNOX POLK

(Eleventh President of the United States)

Last Day in Office: March 4, 1849, after one term.

Background: Said to be humorless, Polk proved to be a hard-working chief executive. He mastered the acquisition of California, ceded to the United States in 1848 by the Treaty of Guadalupe Hidalgo. Polk was very proud of this, though it took a war with Mexico to first conquer the Golden State. Under Polk's administration the Oregon question was settled with a permanent northwestern boundary that was established at the Forty-ninth Parallel.

Of all the U.S. presidents, Polk was the most rigid in his personal life, forbidding such pastimes as card playing, dancing, and drinking anything stronger than tea in the White House. The office of the presidency might have cost him his health. He developed serious diarrhea during his second year in office but ignored his physician's advice to slow down. He was fortunate to have a loving, devoted wife.

Last Day of Life: James Polk died on June 15, 1849.

Background: Less than three months after he left the presidency, James Polk, at age fifty-three, was a physically broken man. While cataloging books in his library, he gave little attention to a seething fever until it overwhelmed him. Bedridden in the last days of his life, he spoke his last words to his wife, Sarah: "I love you, Sarah, for all eternity, I love you." Shortly before he died (he had contracted cholera) on June 15, 1849, in Nashville, Tennessee, his aged mother came into the room, knelt at his bed, and prayed. Joined by his wife and his son, James

Knox Polk slipped away as his wife wept. He was born in Mecklenburg, North Carolina, on November 2, 1795.

Gravesite: State Capitol, Nashville, Tennessee.

ZACHARY TAYLOR
(Twelfth President of the United States)

Last Day of Life: Zachary Taylor died on July 9, 1850, having served as president since March 4, 1849.

Background: Suffering from intestinal disorders, on July 4, 1850, President Taylor aggravated his condition by spending the better part of Independence Day under a broiling Washington, D.C., sun. He continuously satisfied his thirst with iced milk and iced water. Taylor also munched on green apples, cherries, and pieces of raw cabbage. On July 5, not feeling well, the president carried on with his duties, including writing thank-you letters and answering invitations of various kinds.

Aware that he was not feeling well, the sixty-five-year-old president's physician gave him calomel and opium. By the end of the day, the president was ordered to bed, his body overtaken by fever. Fighting back for four days, his stamina quit as the bilious fever produced a vomiting spasm. Doses of quinine were of no use; at 10 o'clock in the evening of July 9, 1850, the failing president awakened from a restless sleep to speak his last words: "Very, but the storm, in passing, has swept away the trunk ... I am about to die—I expect the summons soon—I have endeavored to discharge all my official duties faithfully—I regret nothing, but I am sorry that I am about to leave my friends." His wife and relatives surrounded his bed, and the president was at total peace, his face calm and resigned, when suddenly his eyes closed. President Zachary Taylor expired at 10:33 in the evening. He was born on November 24, 1784, in Virginia.

America's twelfth president is famous for defeating Santa Anna at Buena Vista, though as chief executive he is hardly remembered, having served too briefly.

Gravesite: Zachary Taylor National Cemetery, Louisville, Kentucky.

MILLARD FILLMORE
(Thirteenth President of the United States)

Last Day in Office: March 4, 1853. Millard Fillmore became the thirteenth U.S. president upon the death of Zachary Taylor, who died while in office

Background: The last of the Whig Party presidents, President Fillmore passed into office and out almost unnoticed, and today is regarded as an insignificant president, yet his signing of the Fugitive Slave Act infuriated abolitionists and fueled the growing enmity between the North and the South. Ten years later the Fugitive Slave Act would be used as one of the reasons for South Carolina's secession from the Union. Future secession of Southern states would eventually lead to the Civil War as President Lincoln, trying to preserve the Union at all costs, sought volunteer troops on April 17, 1861, declaring an insurrection as seven states formed the Confederate States of America.

As President, Fillmore held to the Monroe Doctrine favoring nonintervention in the disputes of foreign nations. He sought the presidency as a Whig candidate in 1852 but was unsuccessful. Fillmore was a humble man and even turned down an honorary degree from England's Oxford University, believing such degrees should be awarded to qualified persons. He saw no reason to accept the honor since he had not attended college. In 1856 he ran for the presidency as a Knownothing. He was unsuccessful.

CRIMEAN WAR

Last Day: The Crimean War ended on February 1, 1856.

Background: The Crimean War was started by Russia against Turkey, France, England, and Sardinia. The Crimean War ended on February 1, 1856, when Russia yielded to an Austrian ultimatum, agreeing to a preliminary peace. Russia's Czar Nicholas I declared war on the sultan of Turkey after the sultan refused to make Russia the protector of Orthodox Christians. The war gets its name Crimean from the Crimea, a vast territory in Russia's Ukraine region, where Britain and France sent troops out of distrust of Russia's intentions. The Crimean War is remembered for its famous Light Brigade Charge—a British cavalry charge at Balaklava, Russia on October 25, 1854, and for the heroic work of English nurse and administrator Florence Nightingale (1820–1910). With the peace treaty signed March 30, 1856, France and Great Britain ceased to claim the Turks were "barbarians," an opinion held since the Crusades. Alfred, Lord Tennyson's eloquent poem, "The Charge of the Light Brigade," seems to have added to the significance of the Crimean War, which lasted two years.

FRANKLIN PIERCE
(Fourteenth President of the United States)

Last Day in Office: March 4, 1857, after one term.

Background: Franklin Pierce came to the White House under a pall of sadness, having seen all his children die before maturity. His wife wore black throughout his presidency, which boasted some worthy goals but few accomplishments. Under his presidency the Kansas-Nebraska Act was passed, which he signed in 1854, allowing both territories to decide whether to be free or slave states on the basis of popular sovereignty. This issue was hotly contested because it repealed the Missouri Compromise of 1820, which had been designed to halt the westward spread of slave power. Abolitionists and Northerners were outraged. A civil war erupted in 1855 in Kansas, and by the next year John Brown, obsessed with the idea of ending slavery, massacred several proponents of slavery. President Pierce made many enemies by signing the

Kansas-Nebraska Act, and by the end of his term he was very unpopular.

FAUSTIN SOULOUQUE

Last Monarch of Haiti: Emperor Faustin Soulouque. The emperor came to power in 1849 and reigned until 1859. Thereafter the nation became a republic.

JAMES BUCHANAN
(Fifteenth President of the United States)

Last Day in Office: March 4, 1861, after one term.

Background: James Buchanan is the only U.S. president not to have married. Indeed, his presidency is hardly remembered. He attempted to admit Kansas into the Union as a slave state. He liked fine food, presents, lots of undisturbed sleep, and disliked too much work. He had two friends in his life: himself and the stock market and gave each his utmost personal attention.

NORTH CAROLINA

Last State to Secede from the Union: North Carolina seceded on May 20, 1861.

Background: Other states who left the Union at the outset of the Civil war were South Carolina, Mississippi, Tennessee, Alabama, Virginia, Florida, Texas, Georgia, Louisiana, and Arkansas. The last of the states to return was Georgia, on July 15, 1870.

PONY EXPRESS

Last Day: The Pony Express made its last journey on October 24, 1861, some eighteen months after its inauguration in 1860.

Background: Postal rates were from $2 to $10 per ounce, and well-paid horsemen made deliveries between St. Joseph, Missouri, and Sacramento, California. The entire journey consisted of 1,900 miles, with relay stations every twelve miles. Contending with Indians and outlaws was not easy, but the demise of the service came because of the new Western Union telegraph lines. Private investors lost $200,000.

JOHN TYLER
(Tenth President of the United States)

Last Day of Life: John Tyler died on January 18, 1862.

Background: The former president, in Richmond, Virginia, suffering from a bilious fever, was being attended by a physician when he said: "Doctor, I'm going . . . please, it is best." They were his last words, for as the physician was replying, "I hope not," his patient fell suddenly still, having expired on January 18, 1862. Born March 29, 1790, in Charles City County, Virginia, he was seventy-one years old.

Gravesite: Hollywood Cemetery, Richmond, Virginia.

MARTIN VAN BUREN
(Eighth President of the United States)

Last Day of Life: Martin Van Buren died on July 24, 1862.

Background: Martin Van Buren said his last words, "There is but one reliance," at his Kinderhook estate in New York before he lapsed into a coma and died on July 24, 1862. Born on December 5, 1782, Kinderhook, New York, he was seventy-nine years old when he died due to asthma.

Gravesite: Kinderhook, New York.

BATTLE OF GETTYSBURG

Last Day: The Civil War battle was concluded on July 3, 1863, after the famous mile-long charge by fifteen thousand Confederate troops—the Army of Northern Virginia—against Cemetery Ridge, a charge that ended in a costly bloody failure.

Background: The Confederate soldiers, under the command of General George Pickett, attacked from their own position on Seminary Ridge after a blistering shell assault with a line of 140 cannons had failed to score even one strike against the Union lines. The Union Army of the Potomac, under the command of Major General George Meade, greeted the 3 P.M. Confederate charge against their stronghold with close-range cannon fire. Hundreds of Southern soldiers were killed outright in the face of the endless cannon barrage.

But the Confederate onslaught was marked by Southern courage as hundreds of soldiers reached the summit of the Northern stronghold. A pitched battle of hand-to-hand engagement with muskets, knives, and fists followed. But the bugle for retreat sounded as the Confederate command saw themselves outflanked. The Southern charge against Cemetery Ridge was the South's last chance for a major victory. Lincoln sent dispatches to Major General Meade ordering him to pursue the retreating Confederate Army, but the battle that had begun on July 1 had exhausted the Union forces and inflicted a heavy loss of life on both sides. Nevertheless, had Meade been able to carry out Lincoln's orders, the Civil War would have ended. Never had so many soldiers died in a battle on the North American continent as at the Battle of Gettysburg. Union losses: 3,155 killed, 14,259 wounded, and 5,365 missing or captured. Confederate losses: 3,903 killed, 18,735 wounded, and 5,425 missing or captured. The Battle of Gettysburg was the turning point in the Civil War, the beginning of the end for General Lee and the South. President Lincoln dedicated a national cemetery on the site soon thereafter.

AMERICAN CIVIL WAR

Last Day: On April 9, 1865, Confederate General Robert E. Lee surrendered to Union General Ulysses S. Grant at Appomattox, Virginia.

Background: The Civil War began on April 12, 1861, when Confederate soldiers fired on Fort Sumter in Charleston, South Carolina. The cause: Certain Southern states had threatened to secede from the Union—a Union that President Abraham Lincoln sought to preserve at all costs. The head of the Union forces was General Ulysses S. Grant. Confederate troops were commanded by General Robert E. Lee and were defeated after a cruel and divisive war that pitted brother against brother. The signing of the peace treaty between Grant and Lee took place at Appomattox, Virginia. Union losses in the war were 360,222; Confederate losses, 258,000. The first Union guns fired from Fort Sumter in response to the Confederate salvo were fired by Captain Abner Doubleday—the man who allegedly invented the game of baseball.

ABRAHAM LINCOLN
(Sixteenth President of the United States)

Last Day of Life: Abraham Lincoln was assassinated on April 15, 1865, early into his second term as president.

Background: The tragedy that ended the life of Abraham Lincoln began on Good Friday, April 14, 1865. Confederate sympathizer John Wilkes Booth, member of a prominent theatrical family, entered Ford's Theatre in Washington, D.C., unchallenged, where above, in the dress circle, President Lincoln and his wife sat watching a comedic play, *Our American Cousin*. Moving to door seven, Booth noticed the customary president's security guard had vacated his post. Through a small peephole, Booth was able to observe Lincoln's hand. He also saw another couple, a Major Rathbone and his fiancée.

At approximately 10:13 P.M., as the audience of more than a thousand patrons was laughing at the line "You sockdolagized old mantrap," spoken on stage by an actor named Asa Trenchard, Booth passed into the dress circle. His hand gripping a small brass derringer, he aimed the pistol at the president's temple just as Lincoln was turning his head from the stage to the audience below. Booth fired at the president at point-blank range. Lincoln slumped forward. Mrs. Lincoln leaped to her husband's side. Major Rathbone sprang to his feet, challenging Booth. Slashing at Rathbone with a knife, Booth managed to find the railing of the box, bracing against it as he vaulted beyond to the stage.

It was an awkward descent, as Booth's boot spur became caught in a flag and his shinbone snapped. Before the surprised audience, Booth waved his dagger in triumph, declaring, "*Sic semper tyrannis!*" ("Thus always to tyrants," the motto of Virginia). He staggered off stage and out of the theater.

A young physician was hurried to the dying president's side. An on-the-spot examination revealed a wound in the back of the president's head, just behind his left ear. The president was carefully removed from the theater to a boardinghouse across the street. The next day, Holy Saturday, while a small gathering surrounded his bed, praying softly, Lincoln expired at 7:22 in the morning. The date was April 15. President Abraham Lincoln was fifty-six years old. He had been born on the Nolin River, three miles south of Hodgenville, Kentucky, on February 12, 1809. "With malice toward none; with charity for all . . . " (from Lincoln's second inaugural address).

Known as "Honest Abe," Lincoln's kind, yet sad face became a symbol of the Civil War fought during his administration. Abraham Lincoln epitomized what we expect from our presidents—courage, honesty and leadership. The Civil War is remembered for such bloody battles as Gettysburg, Vicksburg, Fredericksburg, and brave warriors on both sides that are not forgotten—General Lee, General Grant and William T. Sherman. We remember Lincoln today as a man with a beard, a stove-pipe-hat and warm penetrating eyes, for his great Gettysburg Address, for his desire to end slavery and preserve the Union.

Gravesite: Old Ridge Cemetery, Springfield, Illinois.

ALASKA

Last Day Russia Owned Alaska: On April 9, 1867, the sale of Alaska—at two cents an acre—was ratified by the United States, with the transfer of the territory to its new owners to take place on October 18, 1867.

Background: The purchase of the great northern arctic wilderness known as Russian America was arranged by U.S. Secretary of State William H. Seward on March 30, 1867, at a price of $7.2 million. At the time, many U.S. critics had misgivings about the transaction, calling the purchase Seward's Folly. In 1896 gold was discovered in the Klondike region of Alaska. In 1968 oil and natural gas were discovered in Alaska's Prudhoe Bay region. Alaska has paid untold dividends to the United States, for aside from being rich in natural resources (fish, coal, timber, natural gas, and oil into the billions of dollars), its military value to the United States is immeasurable.

One can only wonder in whose hands Alaska would be today if Seward had not survived an assassination attempt. Seward was the secretary of state during Lincoln's second term as president; marked for assassination along with Lincoln, he survived a knife wound inflicted by a Booth cohort the night Lincoln was shot (April 14, 1865)—two years before he proposed Alaska's purchase from Russia.

YOSHINOBU

Last Shogun of Japan: Yoshinobu, of the Tokugawa Shogunate, was forced to abdicate in November 1867, after he was unable to expel foreigners from the country.

Background: The shogun was the actual ruler of Japan, wielding absolute power while an emperor ruled nominally. The Tokugawa Shogunate had ruled Japan for more than 250 years (since 1614). The role of shogun, unique in Japan, began in the twelfth century with the rise of the feudal system, under the Minamoto family. Their commander, Yoritomo, took the title shogun (commander-in-chief). The Meiji Restoration, giving total power to the emperor, replaced Japan's last shogun. The nation is now ruled by a constitution, with a diet, or parliament.

JAMES BUCHANAN

(Fifteenth President of the United States)

Last Day of Life: James Buchanan died on June 1, 1868.

Background: Known as the president who never married, James Buchanan had one medical problem after another. His eyes bothered him, he had glandular illnesses, and he suffered from gout. He was known to be parsimonious, and even as he lay dying, his concerns were for practical matters. He busily gave instructions to have certain stocks bought and sold while the market was good. He also left instructions not to have parades and pomp after his death, and requested that only an inexpensive white headstone and nothing more was to be provided. He once became enraged when a friend wired him collect—the telegram costing $26.80.

On June 1, 1868, at his home in Lancaster, Pennsylvania, as death was near, in the presence of a friend, he promised that history would vindicate anything unfavorable in his presidency. With a last prayer, "O Lord God Almighty, as Thou wilt," he died. The cause of death was rheumatic gout. Born in Cove Gasp, Pennsylvania on April 23, 1791, he was seventy-seven years old.

Gravesite: Woodward Hill Cemetery, Lancaster, Pennsylvania.

ANDREW JOHNSON
(Seventeenth President of the United States)

Last Day in Office: March 4, 1869. Andrew Johnson became the seventeenth United States president upon the assassination of Abraham Lincoln.

Background: Andrew Johnson shocked Congress when he took office by ignoring the ideals and policies of his slain predecessor, including vetoing legislation that would have granted basic rights to blacks. He infuriated Congress when he dismissed Secretary of War Edwin Stanton, who refused to be dismissed. Impeachment proceedings against Johnson resulted, and he won acquittal by one vote.

Johnson was a stubborn man always aching for a fight. He lacked formal education; when he married at age eighteen, his wife became his mentor and teacher. He made much of the fact that he was a poor boy from Tennessee, and as president was gentle and conciliatory, granting pardons to the Confederate rank and file. Johnson was also a president who was not afraid of controversy. He endorsed the purchase of Alaska on the advice of Secretary of State William Seward—an acquisition considered unwise at the time. He came to the presidency at a difficult time in America—a Southerner at a time when a Southern sympathizer had slain Lincoln. Yet the man who many believed was unsuited for the presidency moved toward restoring the Union of States by pardoning the Confederates, which helped heal Southern wounds. Being a Southerner, President Andrew Johnson was the right man at the right time, for the South needed an ally.

FRANKLIN PIERCE
(Fourteenth President of the United States)

Last Day of Life: Franklin Pierce died on October 8, 1869.

Background: Retired and living in Concord, New Hampshire, and suffering from dropsy and a stomach infection, President Pierce had spent his last years in loneliness. His wife, whom he adored, had died in 1863, and Pierce had begun to drink. On October 8, 1869, at dawn, in great pain from stomach inflamation, President Pierce died. Born in Hillsboro, New Hampshire on November 23, 1804, he was sixty-four years old.

Gravesite: Old North Cemetery, Concord, New Hampshire.

MILLARD FILLMORE
(Thirteenth President of the United States)

Last Day of Life: Millard Fillmore died on March 8, 1874.

Background: Retired from public life and living in Buffalo, New York, President Fillmore said his last words to his attending physician on March 8, 1874: "The nourishment was palatable." Suffering from paralysis and having gone into a coma, Millard Fillmore expired at 11 in the evening. Born in Locke, New York, on January 7, 1800, he was seventy-four years old.

Gravesite: Forest Lawn Cemetery, Buffalo, New York.

YOUNGER BROTHERS—BOB, COLE, AND JAMES

Last Successful Robbery: The Pacific-Missouri railroad train on July 7, 1875, near Otterville, Missouri, was the target of the Younger brothers, and the take was $75,000.

ANDREW JOHNSON
(Seventeenth President of the United States)

Last Day of Life: Andrew Johnson died on July 31, 1875.

Background: As Andrew Johnson, the former president and then senator from Tennessee, sat with his granddaughter on the banks of the Watauga River, Carter County, Tennessee, he was at peace. It was a beautiful day, July 30, 1875. His granddaughter was soon to be married, and Johnson looked forward to the wedding. Suddenly, as if hit with a heavy object from behind, Johnson moaned and fell back, struck with apoplexy. Doctors could do nothing to save him, and on July 31, as he lingered near death, his last wish was: "When I die, I desire no better winding sheet than the Stars and Stripes, and no softer pillow than the Constitution." Late that day, the seventeenth president of the United States died. Born on December 29, 1808, in Raleigh, North Carolina, he was sixty-six years old.

Gravesite: Andrew Johnson National Historic Site, Greenville, Tennessee.

PIUS XII

Last Pope Born in the City of Rome: Pope Pius XII was born in Rome on March 2, 1876. He reigned from 1939 until his death on October 2, 1958.

ALEXANDER GRAHAM BELL

Last Experiment in the Invention of the Telephone: On March 10, 1876, at his laboratory in Boston, Massachusetts, the Scottish inventor Alexander Graham Bell put two drops of concentrated sulfuric acid in water, causing the water to act as a conductor for transmitting sound.

Background: Bell spoke into a receiver. His assistant, Thomas Augustus Watson, stationed in an adjacent room, happened to be dozing when he was suddenly alarmed to hear Bell's voice coming over the wire. The first complete sentence transmitted by voice over a wire was: "Mr. Watson, come here. I want you." (Bell had accidentally spilled some acid on himself.) Responding to the command, Watson repeated the sentence to Bell, word for word. The telephone was born.

GEORGE ARMSTRONG CUSTER

Custer's Last Stand: On June 25, 1876, General George Armstrong Custer was defeated at Little Bighorn.

Background: General Custer led 267 soldiers of the U.S. Seventh Cavalry against the Sioux Indians led by Chief Crazy Horse at the Little Bighorn River in Montana, and was soundly defeated on June 25, 1876. The last man standing, the "boy general" with yellow hair who dressed in the buckskin clothes of a frontiersman, was wounded, surrounded by dead horses and men. Custer shot himself rather than face mutilation by the Sioux. The event came to be known as Custer's Last Stand.

YOUNGER BROTHERS—BOB, COLE, AND JAMES

Last Robbery Attempt: At the First National Bank of Northfield, Minnesota, on August 7, 1876, all the Younger brothers were wounded in an ambush by the townspeople. They were captured and given life prison sentences. Jim Younger was eventually paroled and took his own life in 1902. Bob Younger died of tuberculosis in August

1889 while serving his term. Cole Younger died of natural causes in March 1916.

ULYSSES SIMPSON GRANT
(Eighteenth President of the United States)

Last Day in Office: March 4, 1877, after two terms.

Background: Grant was once arrested for driving his carriage too fast, but no charges were pressed when officials discovered that he was the president (though he had asked for no special treatment). Grant was a poor judge of character; some of his cabinet appointments—his secretary of the treasury, secretary of the navy, vice presidents in both his terms, and a minister to Britain—became involved in corruption. He loved animals, and he wept when his daughter, Nellie, was married. He enjoyed cavorting with the rich who bestowed expensive presents on him and his family. He liked whiskey and cigars, and one report claims that he smoked thirty cigars a day. He did not like military pomp such as parades and had no love of politics. The famous picture of Grant wrapped in blankets in his final days, trying to keep warm, aroused the nation to take steps to provide for its presidents after they had left the White House.

THOMAS EDISON

Last Material Used to Invent the Light Bulb: After almost six thousand kinds of materials were used unsuccessfully, on October 21, 1879, Edison found what he was looking for. He used a loop of cotton thread saturated with lampblack, baked in a carbonizing oven more than fifteen hours and then burned inside a vacuum. The cotton burned inside the vacuum for forty-five hours and the light bulb was born.

MASSACRE OF WOUNDED KNEE

Last Day: The massacre of Indians at Wounded Knee ended on December 29, 1880.

Background: The confrontation at Wounded Knee, South Dakota, began when two hundred Indian men, women, and children were rounded up from the Badlands by Seventh Cavalry soldiers after the death of their chief, Sitting Bull. Sitting Bull had been shot and killed when Indian police sought to arrest him. Famous (along with Chief Crazy Horse) for his connection with the Battle of the Little Bighorn in which George Armstrong Custer and his men of the Seventh Cavalry were massacred, Sitting Bull had not participated in the actual battle, for he was making medicine at the time.

Upon the death of Sitting Bull, the Indians began to flee the reservation, which was illegal; they were supposed to remain on their reservations. The Indians opposed to white settlement were rounded up and were being disarmed when a commotion arose. An Indian pulled a gun and wounded a soldier. The incident, which took place at a creek called Wounded Knee, touched off one of the bloodiest massacres of the Indian Wars. The Indians were dressed in their "bulletproof" ghost shirts, believing they were protected from harm; the soldiers, bitter over the massacre at the Little Bighorn, exploded with rage. When the shooting was over, all two hundred Indians, down to the last child, were dead.

Later, at a court of inquiry, the soldiers testified that their vision had been impaired by Indian medicine dust and that they had acted in self-defense. Leaving the scene of the carnage, the soldiers returned the following day to find the corpses blanketed with snow. The dead were buried in a common grave. The Battle of Wounded Knee was the last battle of the Indian Wars.

RUTHERFORD BIRCHARD HAYES
(Nineteenth President of the United States)

Last Day in Office: March 4, 1881, after one term.

Background: Rutherford B. Hayes is considered a mediocre president serving during a relatively uneventful period in U.S. history. Against serving alcoholic drinks in the White House, Hayes is also remembered for urging civil service reform and for his conciliatory position regarding the South—for the Civil War was still a recent memory.

JESSE JAMES

Last Stagecoach Holdup: On March 9, 1881, Jesse James, with his brother Frank and Dick Liddel, Bill Ryan, and Edward Miller, succeeded in holding up a stagecoach near Muscle Shoals, Alabama, and netted just over $1,000.

BILLY THE KID

Last Homicide: Billy's last homicide was the shotgun murder of Warden Robert W. Ollinger at the Mesilla, New Mexico, jail on April 28, 1881. "The Kid" even made good his escape. Ollinger may have been Billy's last, but he was also his twenty-first murder victim.

Background: One of the fastest guns the Old West would ever see, Billy the Kid was wanted for at least twenty-one murders and numerous bank robberies. A hero and a legend to school boys and girls of the day, Billy as a youth worked on the vast New Mexico ranch of John Tunstall, whom he greatly admired. When Tunstall was murdered by cattle rustlers, Billy seems to have lost faith in the good of humanity. Taking the law into his own hands, he tracked down Tunstall's murderers and killed them. Killing became easy, and before long his reputation went to his head. He started taking on law officers entrusted with the duty of apprehending him, killing many of them until a price was put on his head. His real name was William H. Bonney.

JESSE JAMES

Last Bank Robbery: With his brother Frank James and cohorts Bill Ryan, Dick Liddel, and Richard Miller, Jesse James robbed the Davis and Sexton Bank in Riverton, Iowa, on July 10, 1881.

BILLY THE KID

Last Day of Life: On July 15, 1881, in New Mexico, Sheriff Pat Garrett crept up to Billy's hideout, the Maxwell Ranch outside Fort Sumner.

What happened will really never be known, beyond the fact that Billy the Kid's killing days were soon to be over. Of the shots that rang out in the dark night, a single bullet from Garrett's six-shooter through Billy's heart was the fatal one. Born 1859 in New York City, Billy was twenty-one years old.

JESSE JAMES

Last Homicide: Jesse James killed railroad passenger Frank McMillan and engineer William Westphal when, with brother Frank, he held up a Pacific Railroad Express train near the town of Winston, Missouri, on July 15, 1881.

Last Train Robbery: With brother Frank and Charles Ford, Dick Liddel, Clarence Rite, and Wood Rite, Jesse James robbed the Chicago-Alton Express Train on August 7, 1881, taking $1,500 and gold and jewels.

JAMES ABRAM GARFIELD

(Twentieth President of the United States)

Last Day of Life: James A. Garfield was assassinated on September 19, 1881, during his first term as president.

Background: President Garfield died as the result of an assassin's bullet fired months before at a railroad station in Washington, D.C. The tragic day was July 2, 1881, at the Baltimore and Potomac Railroad Station, where the president was planning to journey to his alma mater, Williams College in Massachusetts. As security people were leading the president through the ladies' waiting room, at 9:20 A.M., a man named Charles J. Guiteau, a disappointed office seeker holding a British-made Bull-dog revolver, fired two shots into Garfield's back. He died on September 19, 1881. Born on November 19,

1831, in Cuyahoga, Georgia, he was forty-nine years old. James A. Garfield's presidency is remembered for one interesting fact—he so adored General Lew Wallace's book *Ben Hur* that he appointed Wallace ambassador to Turkey. President Garfield was in office only four months.

Gravesite: View Cemetery, Cleveland, Ohio.

JESSE JAMES

Last Day of Life: Jesse James was shot in the back on March 4, 1882.

Background: On March 4, 1882, Jesse James rose from the table of his home in St. Joseph, Missouri, to straighten a picture on the wall. He had been busy planning a bank robbery and probably wanted to stretch his legs. Uncomfortable with the weight of his gunbelt, which had a pair of six-guns, one on each side, he removed it and resumed toying with the picture. In the room with Jesse were the Ford brothers, Robert (Bob) and Charles. Robert had his eye on the $10,000 reward for Jesse, dead or alive, so he eased his six-gun from his holster and shot Jesse James twice from behind, killing the Old West's most famous bank robber.

Born in 1847, James was thirty-four years old when he died. Jesse's brother, Frank, was tried for the killing, but was acquitted. Frank died of natural causes on February 2, 1915. Robert Ford never received the full $10,000 reward and was shot to death by Ed Kelly at Creeds, Colorado, on July 8, 1892. His brother Charles Ford took his own life some years later.

BELLE STARR

Last Robbery: Belle Starr stole horses in 1883, for which the outlaw drew a six-month prison sentence.

BATTLE OF KHARTOUM

Last Day: The battle's last day was January 26, 1885, when General Charles Gordon, leading Sudanese troops, was massacred at Khartoum (Sudan) by the Mahdi's forces in one of the bloodiest battles for control of the Sudan.

Background: With the annihilation of General Hicks Pasha and his ten-thousand-man force by the Mahdists on November 4, 1883, Gordon, a British soldier, cadet, and hero, was sent to the Sudan to rescue and evacuate the European and Egyptian population. Gordon was approved and given executive powers by Egypt's Khedive Mohammed Tewfil. The fanatical Mahdi (the Guided One), who claimed to have a divine mission to lead a holy war against infidels, vowed not to let the Egyptians leave Khartoum.

For nine months General Gordon battled the Mahdi's soldiers, while managing to evacuate more than three thousand Egyptian men, women, and children. Though he put up a good fight, for Gordon the end was near. He had been surrounded and trapped in Khartoum since March 12, 1884. A stubborn, indecisive British government complicated the dire situation by delaying the order to send reinforcements. When they did arrive, it was too late. The fatal day had come and gone. Khartoum had fallen on January 26, 1885, and with it General Gordon, his head impaled on a spear as a trophy for the victors. The Mahdi passed away mysteriously on June 21 of that same year. Khartoum was retaken by the British in 1898. Gordon was buried in the Sudan, a land he felt was worth dying for.

CHESTER ALAN ARTHUR
(Twenty-first President of the United States)

Last Day in Office: March 4, 1885. Chester Alan Arthur became the twenty-first president upon the assassination of James Garfield.

Background: President Arthur did not receive the nomination of his party for reelection. The man who came to the presidency upon the death of Garfield was quite astonished and fearful of the office. But as vice president, Arthur was the only man the nation could turn to, and with bravery he took the plunge. His cronies back in New York expected him to kowtow to their wishes. He did not. Arthur turned over a new leaf. He fought pork-barrel legislation and improved the civil service. He also worked for a stronger navy and had postage rates reduced. Arthur might have found it hard to be a good politician today because he refused to kiss babies or give interviews to nosy reporters who sought to probe his private life.

ULYSSES SIMPSON GRANT
(Eighteenth President of the United States)

Last Day of Life: Ulysses S. Grant died on July 23, 1885.

Background: Grant suffered from malignant throat cancer, which was discovered too late to remedy. The trouble had begun in the back of Grant's tongue and in his tonsils and was diagnosed as carcinoma. With the help of Mark Twain, Grant struggled to write his memoirs, because he badly needed the money for his family. As July 23, 1885, dawned, Grant was thin and frail, but he had managed to write the final pages of his book. In a cottage in Saratoga Springs, New York, in the early morning, Grant struggled to speak a last word: "Water." At 8:05 in the morning, Grant let out a long sigh, and the former president and Civil War general was dead. Born on April 27, 1822, at Point Pleasant, Ohio, he was sixty-three years old.

Gravesite: Grant's Tomb, New York City.

CHESTER ALAN ARTHUR
(Twenty-first President of the United States)

Last Day of Life: Chester A. Arthur died on November 18, 1886.

Background: On November 16, 1886, President Arthur visited with his sisters in his New York home and was in jovial spirits, sharing childhood memories. Upon retiring for bed that night, President Arthur lapsed into unconsciousness due to a cerebral hemorrhage. He never fully regained consciousness, dying peacefully on the morning of November 18, 1886. Born in

Fairfield, Vermont, on October 5, 1830, he was fifty-six years old.

Gravesite: Albany Rural Cemetery, Albany, New York.

BELLE STARR

Last Day of Life: On February 3, 1889, Belle Starr was shot to death by an unknown assailant while riding on a trail near Briartown, Montana. Some historians believe that Belle Starr's son and sometime lover, eighteen-year-old Eddie Reed, killed her. Survived by a daughter, Pearl, she was born Myra Belle Shirley in Carthage, Missouri. She was forty-one years old.

PEDRO II

Last Monarch of Brazil: Pedro II of Brazil abdicated on November 15, 1889, and gave way to a republic form of government.

Background: Pedro II succeeded his father, Pedro I, who had abdicated (in 1831). Pedro II's actual reign began in 1840, and though he was a popular emperor, discontent eventually set in among the people, leading to his abdication.

DALTON BROTHERS—BOB, GRAT, AND EMMIT

Last Bank Robbery: On the fateful day of October 5, 1892, in the early morning, Bob, Grat, and Emmit Dalton, with Dick Broadwell and Billy Powers, entered the town of Coffeyville, Kansas, intent on robbing two banks—Condon and the First National Bank—at the same time.

Background: As they arrived in Coffeyville, the five outlaws were seen with their .45s and Winchesters, and an alert went out to the townspeople. At 10:15 A.M. Powers, Broadwell, and Grat Dalton emerged from the Condon Bank with less than $2,000 in paper money. At the same time Bob and Emmit Dalton were at the First National Bank, collecting money from a teller who was being uncooperative, when gunfire from angry townspeople shattered the windows. Scurrying from the bank through a back door, Bob Dalton shot and killed two townspeople. He also took the time to go back into the bank and kill the uncooperative bank clerk who started it all. With bullets rattling at their feet, the two Dalton brothers raced in the direction of their mounts tied up in an alley. In the mad scramble they managed to bring down some of their pursuers. Once in the alley they found their brother Grat with Powers and Broadwell. They knew they were trapped. Grat Dalton decided to take on the town marshal, and they both lost their lives in the exchange of shots.

With little cover, the bandits were forced to shoot it out with the townspeople. Powers fell before he could get his foot in the stirrup on his saddle. Broadwell had barely mounted his skittish horse when he was struck with bullets as he was carried through a raging gauntlet of blazing guns; he was dead before he reached the town limits. Bob Dalton, grappling with his spinning horse, was unable to grab its reins as the horse pulled away from him, leaving him out in the open and an easy target. In the throes of death, Bob Dalton said his last words to his brother Emmit: "Don't surrender, die game." But Emmit, wounded, had no recourse but to submit. He was sentenced to life imprisonment but was paroled in 1931.

RUTHERFORD BIRCHARD HAYES
(Nineteenth President of the United States)

Last Day of Life: Rutherford B. Hayes died on January 17, 1893.

Background: Suffering from heart disease, President Hayes spoke his last words: "I know that I am going where Lucy [his wife] is." Death came to Hayes at his home in Fremont, Ohio, on January 17, 1893. He was seventy years old. Hayes was born in Delaware, Ohio, on October 4, 1822.

Gravesite: Oakwood Cemetery, Fremont, Ohio.

BENJAMIN HARRISON

(Twenty-third President of the United States)

Last Day in Office: March 4, 1893, after one term.

Background: Benjamin Harrison was the grandson of the ninth United States president, William Henry Harrison. Benjamin Harrison lost the popular vote and yet became president after the Electoral College vote, by sixty-five electoral votes. He is only one example of why over the years the power of the Electoral College has made many American voters cynical about voting for presidents.

His campaign was supported by big business, which accused his opponent, Grover Cleveland, of being an enemy of the free-enterprise system. The public didn't like Harrison, nor did they believe his supporters; they demonstrated this dislike by giving Cleveland the popular vote. Yet Cleveland lost, and Harrison became one of the weakest presidents on record.

The real power in Harrison's administration was said to be a man called the "czar," Thomas Brackett Reed, the Speaker of the House from Maine. Reed liked to spend money—not his own, the taxpayers'. Harrison approved the programs as passed by the House of Representatives ruled by Reed. As his presidency came to a close, the Congress under his administration became known as the Billion Dollar Congress.

LILIUOKALANI

Last Monarch of Hawaii: Queen Liliuokalani was deposed on June 17, 1893, in a bloodless revolution. Her fall brought to an end Hawaiian rule under a monarchy, begun more than one hundred years before with King Kamehameha I.

Background: When her brother, King David Kalakahua, died on January 20, 1891, the former Lydia Kalakahua became Queen Liliuokalani of Hawaii. Queen Liluokalani would have passed into history a forgotten figure were it not for a song she wrote that became world-famous: "Aloha Oe," which means "Farewell to Thee."

GROVER CLEVELAND
(Twenty-second and Twenty-fourth President of the United States)

Last Day in Office: March 4, 1887, after his second nonconsecutive term.

Background: The only U.S. president to be married for the first time while holding the office, Cleveland made Civil War veterans angry by vetoing pensions. He then infuriated unions by sending the army against Chicago's Pullman strikers for impeding the U.S. mails. Friends who supported both his presidencies found him ungrateful. The man who had once sired an illegitimate child, and refused to conceal this fact even if it meant losing the presidency, wanted no part of pork-barrel or machine politics.

Perhaps most important to his presidency was Cleveland's fight for a strong gold standard when many powerful mine interests felt that the future of the United States was in silver. Cleveland thought otherwise and fought to repeal the Silver Purchase Act, which saw the United States wasting its precious gold to buy easily mined silver. Cleveland did not endear himself to business by seeking a lower tariff, but did endear himself to the populace when opposing Great Britain in its boundary dispute with Venezuela. He once lamented, "My God, what is there in this office that any man should ever want to get into it."

Among the presidents, Grover Cleveland was the only one to serve two nonconsecutive terms. Between his first and second terms as chief executive, his daughter, Ruth Cleveland, was born. In 1921 the Curtiss Candy Company, conveniently remembering the popularity of the child (who was affectionately called Baby Ruth by the public), named a candy bar after her. The candy bar sold well, not because it had been inspired by the president's child, but because the public linked its name to the home-run king of the day, Babe Ruth. Curtiss had made the name Baby Ruth its trademark just as Ruth was making the home run his.

SPANISH-AMERICAN WAR

Last Day: December 10, 1898 was the last day of the war, marked by the signing of the Treaty of Paris.

Background: Cuba and Spain were at war over the issue of Cuba's independence from Spain, and the United States did not want to become involved, though she sympathized with Cuba. However, on January 12, 1898, a riot broke out in Havana, Cuba, and to protect American interests, life, and property, President William McKinley ordered the battleship *Maine,* under the command of Captain Charles D. Sigsbee, into Havana Harbor. While the *Maine* was in the harbor on the night of February 15, 1898, with 358 men aboard, an explosion of undetermined origin sank the ship, killing 260 sailors. While a navy court of inquiry was investigating the tragic event, William Randolph Hearst's "yellow press" whipped up support for American involvement in the conflict through prejudiced articles in the *New York Journal,* claiming Spanish agents were responsible for the sinking of the *Maine.* On April 24, 1898, the United States declared war on Spain. One of the famous yet costly battles of the war was the engagement on San Juan Hill in which Spanish troops abandoned their Gatling guns and retreated from the uphill advance of Theodore Roosevelt's troops. The San Juan charge by the future United States President and his Rough Riders cost 230 U.S. Cavalry Volunteers their lives. But the defeat of the Spanish naval fleet off Santiago on July 3, 1898, brought Spain to the peace table, and Spain relinquished all claims to Cuba. The United States lost 380 in battle, and another 5,006 to disease.

VICTORIA

Last Day of Life: Victoria, Queen of Great Britain and Ireland and Empress of India, died on January 22, 1901.

Background: At the time of her death at age eighty-one, Queen Victoria was prepared to lead her nation into the twentieth century. It was not to be. At Osborne House on the Isle of Wight, Britain, after having embraced her elder son, with a last utterance, "Bertie," she fell silent. It was January 22, 1901. At 6 in the evening her heart stopped, ending the reign of England's most beloved monarch. She was born Alexandrina Victoria at Kensington Palace, London, on May 24, 1819.

Probably no queen in history reigned with as much power and a sense of goodwill from her people as did Victoria. She was blessed to have as her prime ministers Lord Melbourne, Lord Palmerston, Benjamin Disraeli, and William Ewart Gladstone, all bright and gifted men who aided her through what was known as England's Victorian Age. At age nineteen Queen Victoria enjoyed what might have been her happiest moment in life on February 10, 1840, when she wed her consort, Prince Albert of Saxe-Coburg-Gotha. Albert not only fathered her nine children but also provided guidance in the affairs of state. There were heartaches during her reign, the Crimean War (1854), for example, and toward the end of her life the Boer War (1898).

Her greatest sorrow was the death of her husband on December 14, 1861, and with his passing, it was said that Victoria's lovely face was never to reveal the sunny smile she had been famous for. Queen Victoria took the English monarchy to its height of popularity by exhibiting dignity and respect for high moral standards and good manners. She was a woman who asked not so much to be served as to serve her empire. With her death, Great Britain mourned the passing of a shining star in the history of the British monarchy.

BENJAMIN HARRISON
(Twenty-third President of the United States)

Last Day of Life: Benjamin Harrison died on March 13, 1901.

Background: At his home in Indianapolis, Indiana, on March 13, 1901, President Harrison, near death, spoke his last words. "Are the doctors here?" he inquired, adding, "Doctor . . . my lungs." At 4:45 in the afternoon death came from pneumonia. Born on August 20, 1833, in North Bend, Ohio, he was sixty-seven years old.

Gravesite: Crown Hill Cemetery, Indianapolis, Indiana.

BUTCH CASSIDY AND THE SUNDANCE KID

Last Confirmed Robbery in the United States: The outlaws got away with $40,000 from the Great Northern Train with other gang members on July 2, 1901, in Wagner, Montana.

Background: Cassidy was born Robert Parker (1886–1908); the Sundance Kid was born Harry Longabaugh (1863–1908). Both Cassidy and Sundance were members of the notorious Wild Bunch Gang, whose hideout was called the "Hole-in-the-Wall." With the gang they managed numerous bank and train robberies and rustled cattle and committed murder. Cassidy got his name "Butch" when he took a job as a meat-cutter in an attempt to leave the outlaw life behind. After their last robbery, the Wild Bunch split up with Cassidy and Sundance riding one way and the rest another way. The pair was last spotted in Mexico in 1908. The Paul Newman/Robert Redford film of their exploits contributed to the legend that they were only happy-go-lucky and harmless bank robbers.

BOXER REBELLION

Last Day: On September 7, 1901, the Peace of Peking was signed, ending the Boxer Rebellion.

Background: The Boxer movement began in the mid-1890s. It was a rebellion in China headed by a secret society called the Society of Harmonious Fists and labeled simply Boxers by foreigners. During the Manchu Dynasty, China's last dynasty, and with the approval of China's last empress, Empress Dowager Tzu Hsi, the Boxers—an antiforeign organization—began to besiege foreign legations on January 20, 1900, and started fifty-five days of fighting and killing on both sides. The main setting of the Boxers' terror campaign was centered around Peking in northern China. Many missionaries, Christians, and the German foreign minister lost their lives. Foreign businesses, homes, and churches were destroyed. The loss of life among the Boxers was substantial, and many innocent civilians not connected to the Boxers were sacrificed to the bloody rebellion.

The Boxer Rebellion ended in a defeat for the Boxers on August 14, 1901, when forces from Japan, Great Britain, Russia, and the United States arrived in Peking. Some 250 foreigners died in the final push to defeat the Boxers. China was forced to pay indemnities to the foreign powers.

WILLIAM McKINLEY
(Twenty-fifth President of the United States)

Last Day of Life: William McKinley was assassinated on September 14, 1901, early into his second term as president.

Background: President McKinley was in Buffalo, New York, to make a speech about commercial exchange among nations at the Pan American Exposition. On September 6, 1901, the day after his appearance at the exposition, the president was greeting guests in a receiving line at the Temple of Music Hall, flanked by Secret Service agents who anxiously urged the greeters to be brief. A young man named Leon Czolgosz, an anarchist, approached the president with a handkerchief resembling a bandage covering his left hand. McKinley extended his hand, but Czolgosz pushed it aside, and the handkerchief suddenly exploded with gunfire.

A dazed expression of horror and surprise on his face, his hands gripping his stomach, the president sighed weakly, "Cortelyou". John Cortelyou was his secretary, standing at his side. Earlier that day he had expressed fears of an assassination attempt. It had happened. Two bullets from a short-barreled .32-caliber Iver Johnson revolver had struck the president; one of the bullets had pierced the wall of McKinley's stomach, and proved to be fatal. The wounded president lingered near death for

more than a week until September 14, at 2:15 A.M. Mc-
Kinley said his last words: "It is God's way. His will be
done, not ours. We are all going, we are all going, oh
dear." Those words pronounced, William McKinley
died. Born January 29, 1843, in Niles, Ohio, he was fifty-
eight years old.

Aside from the fact that President McKinley lost his
life to a mindless assassin, he is remembered for being
a defender of the gold standard. During his presidency
the Spanish-American War was fought and Cuba won its
independence from Spain. Also McKinley sent U.S.
troops to China to help put down a popular uprising
that became known as the Boxer Rebellion.

Gravesite: McKinley Tomb, Canton, Ohio.

BOER WAR

Last Day: The Treaty of Vereeniging officially ended the
Boer War on May 31, 1902.

Background: The Boer War was a conflict between the
Dutch farmers of Cape Colony (now Cape Province) on
the tip of South Africa and Great Britain's numerous
settlers who had taken up residence in South Africa after
gold was discovered in 1885. The war began on October
12, 1899, when the Dutch, led by their president, Oom
Paul Kruger, seized the gold-rich Transvaal town of Ma-
feking, fearing British acquisition of the land. Great Britain won the war largely because of the sheer number of
troops under her command; however, severe jungle conditions and disease resulted in the deaths of many soldiers. In the end, the Boers were permitted to form their
own government. Today they are known as the Afrika-
ners, most of them descendants of German, Dutch, and
Huguenot parents.

THEODORE ROOSEVELT
(Twenty-sixth President of the United States)

Last Day in Office: March 4, 1909, after almost two terms.

Theodore Roosevelt became the twenty-sixth president upon the assassination of William McKinley.

Background: Teddy Roosevelt was famous for many things. He was the youngest man to be elected president of the United States, at age forty-two, and he was the first president to be awarded the Nobel Peace Prize (1906), for persuading Japan to make peace with Russia in the Russo-Japanese War of 1904–1905. He was responsible for seeing that the Panama Canal was built. And he used the power of antitrust laws to dissolve the corporate trusts, establishing a Bureau of Corporations as a watchdog over big business's monopolizing practices.

Having read Upton Sinclair's *The Jungle,* a book about the Chicago stockyards where meat inspectors took bribes and allowed tubercular cattle and hogs to be slaughtered for sale to U.S. butcher shops, Roosevelt pushed for passage of pure food and drug laws to safeguard the public. He was also famous for pithy sayings: "Walk softly and carry a big stick, you will go far." "My hat is in the ring." He popularized the term "muckrakers" to describe writers like Sinclair. Prior to his presidency, Teddy Roosevelt charged up San Juan Hill with his Rough Riders in 1898 in the Battle of San Juan, becoming a folk hero. He had married the former Alice Tahtaway at age twenty-two. Although he tried for a third term as president he was not successful.

MANUEL II

Last Monarch of Portugal: King Manuel II of Portugal abdicated on October 4, 1910, in the face of a revolution.

Background: Manuel (Manoel in Portuguese) II was trained for a naval career. As king, he was forced to flee his throne, eventually settling in England, where in 1913 he married and lived the life of a wealthy gentleman. Born in 1888, Portugal's last king came to the throne upon the assassination of his father. He died in exile in 1932 at age forty-three. Portugal today is a republic.

MANCHU DYNASTY

Last Dynasty of China: The Imperial Manchu Dynasty came to the end with the abdication of Emperor Hsuan-T'ung (Pu-Yi) on February 12, 1912. The Manchus had ruled China since 1644 after an uprising that ended the previous Ming Dynasty.

Background: From Manchuria, northeast China, the Manchu rulers were considered foreigners by the majority of their countrymen, yet they followed a course of moderation upon their ascendancy to power. Both Buddhism and Confucianism remained influential. The sign of Manchu loyalty was the pigtail, worn by all under the law. The last empress of China was Empress Dowager Tzu Hsi, who died in 1908. The last emperor was the Manchu Emperor Henry Pu-Yi, installed by the invading Japanese in 1931.

China was proclaimed a republic when Sun Yat-sen became its first president, soon giving way to Yuan Shih-Kai, who became a dictator and a tyrannical ruler. The last of China's native rulers were the Mings (1368–1644), who brought an end to the Mongol rulers.

Today Ming China, porcelain characterized by blue and white colors with soft floral designs and elegant tall vases, continues to excite the art world and hold great value. Other dynasties of China include the Mongol rulers (1279–1368), fierce nomad tribes led by Genghis Kahn and his grandson, Kublai Kahn; the Sung Dynasty (960–1279), and the T'ang Dynasty (612–906 A.D.) in ancient times: the Han Dynasty (206 B.C.–A.D. 220), and prior to the Han rulers, Shih Huang-Ti, China's first ruler. Today China is called the People's Republic.

ROBERT F. SCOTT

Last Diary Entry: "Thursday 29 March [1912]: Since the 21st we have had a continuous gale from WSW and SW. We had fuel to make two cups of tea a-piece and bare food for two days on the 20th. Every day we have been ready to start for our depot 11 miles away, but outside the door of the tent it remains a scene of whirling drift. I do not think we can hope for any better things now. We shall stick it out to the end, but we are getting weaker, of course, and the end cannot be far. It seems a pity, but I do not think I can write more.

R. Scott

For God's sake look after our people."

Background: Hoping to be the first explorer to reach the South Pole, Robert Falcon Scott, commander of the British expedition, with Petty Officer Edger Evans, Captain L. E. G. Oates, Dr. E. A. Wilson, and Lieutenant H. R. Bowers, began their journey across the inhospitable frozen high polar plateau in November 1911. Each of five sledges (British for sleds) weighed over 190 pounds and contained invaluable scientific equipment and rations. November passed into December, with their rations thinning but their hearts hopeful.

In January 1912 they neared the Pole. On January 18, Captain Scott beheld the disappointing sight of Norwegian flags. The expedition that had begun in 1910 in search of the South Pole—an expedition that had taken years to plan—was defeated. Roald Amundsen and four fellow Norwegians with their seventeen remarkable huskies had arrived at the South Pole a month before, on December 14, 1911. The five explorers had to withdraw on a trek more than eight hundred miles in sub-zero weather through blizzard conditions, descending Beardsmore Glacier after first retreating across the polar plateau.

The journey back home began the very day of their arrival at the Pole. The weather was so fierce that within a month the expedition members were fighting for their lives. Petty Officer Evans died on February 16, after a fall that left him delirious. On March 17 Oates, suffering from frostbite and swollen feet, awakened from an agonizing sleep, threw aside his sleeping bag, and trudged into the blizzard. He was never seen again. Scott wrote in his diary on March 17: "He [Oates] said, 'I am just going outside and may be some time.' " On March 19 the expedition was desperate and a makeshift camp was set up some eleven miles from a provision camp. Nature had stopped them for good. The interminable cold, howling gales, and blasting snow were closing around the little party to entomb them.

On November 12, 1912, the remains of Robert F. Scott and two of his companions, Dr. E. A. Wilson and Lieutenant H. R. Bowers, were found frozen under a high snowdrift. Oates and Evans were never found.

TITANIC

Last Day: The *Titanic* hit an iceberg and sank on April 15, 1912, on her maiden voyage.

> *I cannot imagine any condition which could cause this ship to founder. I cannot conceive of any vital disaster happening to this vessel. Modern ship building has gone beyond that.*
>
> Captain E. J. Smith,
> Master of the Titanic,
> published in the *New York Times*,
> April 16, 1912

Background: It was called the world's greatest sea tragedy, and its root cause was probably plain old ambition. Captain E. J. Smith hoped to set a new speed record for trans-Atlantic crossing. Enroute to New York from Southampton, England, the race was on. With no lookouts posted, with little credence given to messages on her own wireless from the U.S. Atlantic seaboard that icebergs were a threat in the North Atlantic shipping lanes, the *Titanic* flew at a suicidal twenty-two knots.

At 11:37 P.M. on April 14, deep in her bowels, a wrenching, groaning noise was evident to the boiler-room crews feeding the *Titanic*'s 159 furnaces. The four-story vessel, touted for her outstanding appointments—Turkish baths, pools, and vast dining salons—was forging into an iceberg. The phone on the bridge rang. Two minutes went by before the phone was at last picked up, and the ship's wheels turned in a frantic effort to avert disaster. A terrible gnawing sound grew louder just below the *Titanic*'s waterline. The ship's hull had been ruptured. To the merry passengers, the rupture registered as a slight tremor, and perhaps the most annoyance was a spilled drink, a missed step in a waltz. But the "unsinkable" vessel had scraped an iceberg with lethal results. Desperation, panic, and screaming characterized the scene in the boiler rooms and seamen's quarters as the supposedly watertight compartments took in torrents of sea through her torn steel-framed hull. As the vessel began to quake, distress signals sputtered, the radio transmitted the ship's call letters, M G Y.

A ship was in the vicinity. The vessel *Californian* could have come to the *Titanic*'s rescue had its radio receiver been turned on to receive messages. Instead, the *Californian* went about her business, missing a chance to write a glorious chapter into the annals of maritime history. The *Titanic* began to sink and the vessel started to tilt. On her swaying decks, pandemonium erupted over lifeboats that were able to accommodate only a third of the passengers. The instinct for survival knew no bounds, for the traditional unwritten maritime law of sex discrimination that permits women to board the lifeboats ahead of men was violently contested by some of the male passengers. With both crew and passengers at each other's throats, with people rolling and being pitched forward and sliding into the icy depths, with water contaminating the vessel's boilers and producing explosions, the first of the ship's four funnels (smoke stacks) slid into the frigid sea. While lifeboats pulled away from the doomed ship with the fortunate souls, cries of fear echoed into the night, to be remembered forever by those who were saved. A sudden shower of sparks crackled from the port and masthead as the *Titanic*'s lights touched water. The last of her flares were spent, momentarily bathing the night in short-lived brilliance. The vessel began to give up her second, then third funnels to the sea. Strains from the band of "Nearer My God to Thee" faded into the hissing of water. A last explosion was muffled. With a loud roar the great stern of the vessel plunged into the furious swirling sea. The *Titanic* was gone. The time was 2:20 A.M., April 15, 1912.

While silence drew upon the night, the vessel descended sixteen thousand feet to the ocean floor. Two ships had picked up the *Titanic*'s SOS—"We have struck an iceberg. We are damaged. Send help!" The *Virginian* and the *Carpathia,* a Cunard vessel, raced to the scene. Dawn had not yet come when the *Carpathia* arrived. She looked for the great vessel, her captain refusing to believe that the *Titanic* was gone. She found sixteen lifeboats with 711 survivors. If the boats had been filled to capacity, they could have held 928 passengers. Four lifeboats were damaged while being launched, and a total of 1,517 persons died. A court of inquiry found the *Titanic*'s owners guilty of negligence: not enough lifeboats; a crew untrained in safety procedures; and excessive speed in iceberg conditions. The investigation also found unforgivable negligence on the part of the *Californian*'s captain.

WILLIAM HOWARD TAFT

(Twenty-seventh President of the United States)

Last Day in Office: March 4, 1913, after one term.

Background: Cartoonists had a field day at the expense of the twenty-seventh president of the United States, for Taft weighed 362 pounds. As president he is remembered for being good-natured, taking on the trust companies, and failing to cut tariffs, which cost him his popularity. But Taft was too good-natured to lose his sense of humor. He was the first president to throw out a baseball officially opening the baseball season, beginning a tradition. After leaving the presidency, he was chief justice of the U.S. Supreme Court from 1920 until his death.

FRANZ FERDINAND

Last Day of Life: Archduke Franz Ferdinand was assassinated on June 28, 1914, triggering World War I.

Background: The assassination of Archduke Franz Ferdinand and his wife, Sophie, on June 28, 1914, was one of history's most grievous acts. The assassination of the archduke ultimately led to World War I, as it gave Austria the motive for moving against Serbia because the assassin was a Serbian. When he was to go on trial in Serbia, Austria demanded that its officials be able to take part in the proceedings. Serbia balked, insisting the issue be decided by an outside party of international figures. The proud Austro-Hungarian officials refused, and on July 28, 1914, declared war on Serbia. Other European nations came into the conflict—Russia to the aid of Serbia, Germany to Austria-Hungary's side. When France, Great Britain, Italy, and eventually the United States entered the conflict it became known as the Great War.

June 28, 1914, was a lovely Sunday in Sarajevo, capital of Bosnia in central Yugoslavia. Archduke Franz Ferdinand and his consort, Sophie, Duchess of Hohenberg, were in Sarajevo at the invitation of the local military governor, General Potiorek, who had requested that the archduke preside as inspector general of the armed forces. A Serbian secret society known as the Black Hand, a group dedicated to the unification of the southern Slavs, saw the archduke as an obstacle to their goals. No fewer than seven assassins were in the crowd along the parade route known as the Appel Quay. The royal couple was in brilliant regalia, Franz Ferdinand in princely cock's feathers and military tunic, the duchess in a white silk dress and large hat. They sat in an open car waving and responding to the cheers of the crowd, numbered in the thousands. The royal couple were on their way to the town hall where Franz would give a speech during a banquet.

Cool breezes off the River Milaca added to the festival-like atmosphere, but the royal chauffeur was nervous and on the lookout for trouble. Suddenly a hand appeared to wave and threw a bomb, a small contraption that bounced passed Sophie and hit Franz's hand before bounding off the open hood of the car onto the street and to the next car in the procession, where it exploded, leaving it a wreck and injuring its passenger. The assassin, a young high school student named Vaso Cubrilovic, was set upon by the throng and seriously beaten as he attempted to swallow a cyanide tablet.

Of the seven assassins who lined the procession route, all but one fled in panic and were apprehended. The one who stayed in the crowd, Gavrilo Princip, age eighteen, was a nationalist fanatic. The royal couple continued unimpeded to the town hall. As they were returning after the speech, the chauffeur, confused about the originally scheduled route, stopped the car and tried to return to the Appel Quay route. By some strange twist of fate, Princip happened to be only feet from where the archduke's car was halted. As the chauffeur was backing up the auto, Princip burst from the crowd, dashed onto the running board of the car, and with his Russian Browning pistol fired two bullets at the horrified archduke and duchess. Sophie sat upright, motionless, and at first appeared unhurt. She turned to take her husband in her arms as blood spilled from his mouth as a result of the bullet that had pierced his neck. As Sophie began to weep, she suddenly fell forward, dead. The archduke, seized with emotion, cried to his wife, "Sophie! Sophie! Don't die! Keep alive for the children." Sophie died almost immediately from a bullet wound in the abdomen. The archduke began to sink and died moments later. The deaths paved the way for one of the worst wars the world would ever see—World War I.

LUSITANIA

Last Day: The ocean liner *Lusitania* was sunk by German torpedoes on May 7, 1915.

Background: While sailing off the Irish coast on May 7, 1915, on its way from New York, the *Lusitania* was struck by two German torpedoes from a U-20 which inflicted massive holes in her portside. With a complement of 1,198 passengers—among them 128 Americans, including sportsman Alfred G. Vanderbilt and author Justin Forman—the thirty-ton *Lusitania* sank in eighteen minutes in sixty fathoms of sea. It was the first major strike by the German U-boats and a frightening signal of the maliciousness of the German military command, a military that would sink a ship of helpless passengers. Years after, it was revealed that the *Lusitania* was in fact ferrying arms to Great Britain, and therefore was a very likely target.

EASTER REBELLION

Last Day: The last day of the uprising was April 30, 1916, six days after the rebellion broke out on Easter Monday.

Background: The Easter Rebellion did not at first have the popular support of the Irish people. The setting was Dublin, where some two thousand armed men with one day's rations rushed and occupied the General Post Office, four courts, and railroad terminals, demonstrating for the proclamation of the Irish Republic. On Friday and Saturday, April 28 and 29, the British stormed the rebel strongholds, and innocent people and rebels were killed. A message for peace terms, sent by the volunteer leader Patrick Henry Pearse to the British through a Red Cross nurse, was refused. At 2 o'clock in the afternoon of Saturday, April 29, the Irish volunteers surrendered, with Pearse saying, "We surrender in order to prevent further slaughter of unarmed people, and in the hope of saving lives of our fellows, now surrounded and hopelessly outnumbered." But it was not until Sunday, April 30, that all the rebels surrendered. After the Easter Rebellion the British army began a massive roundup of suspected Irish sympathizers.

But what turned Irish fury and hatred against Great Britain was the execution by firing squad of the leaders of the rebellion, including the principal figure, Pearse. Many of those executed were still boys. The executed were seen as martyrs, and their deaths paved the way for continued Irish struggles for independence. With the compromise treaty of December 6, 1921, ratified by the Dail Eireann, or Irish Republic's parliament, by a very narrow majority, the Irish Free State was established. Southern Ireland (the Catholic Irish Free State) embraced twenty-six counties. Six counties with a Protestant majority, the northern counties, remained under British control. The centuries-old conflict for a united Ireland continues, and the bitter memories of the Easter Rebellion fuel the conflict today.

GRIGORY YEFIMOVICH RASPUTIN

Last Day of Life: Rasputin was poisoned, shot, and drowned on December 30, 1916.

Background: Rasputin's influence on the czarina and through her on the czar resulted in unwise appointments to high Russian political posts and was believed to be at the root of Russia's descent into economic chaos. Rasputin was not entirely to blame, but when a rumor spread that he was urging the czarina to make a settlement with the hated Germans, his enemies hatched a dangerous plan to kill the man then known as the Mad Monk.

The plot to do away with Rasputin was designed in St. Petersburg at the Moika Palace where Prince Felix Yussupov lived. The prince (the spouse of the czar's niece) and four others—all zealous Russians—had decided to make their strike on the night of December 30, 1916, while the post-Christmas atmosphere still prevailed.

Toward evening Rasputin, a man with warm and persuasive blue eyes, long hair, and a beard, arrived at the prince's beautiful palace. Though he was a peasant, Rasputin was at home in the presence of royalty. A jovial and cordial mood was manufactured where the prince and several close friends drank and toasted and embraced their guests. When Rasputin had taken several glasses of vintage Madeira, he sang, and with the prince descended the carpeted stairs to a plush basement where finery, paintings, crystal mirrors, and sensual artworks served to distract him. A tray of cakes laced with cyanide was offered and Rasputin ate one, then another, and a third. The prince became concerned because the cyanide-injected cakes failed to have any effect. Rasputin sang and the prince tried to maintain his composure by playing a guitar.

Seized with both fear and courage, the prince laid

down his instrument and sighed with pretentious reverence as he made a gesture to a cross on one wall. Rasputin stopped singing and faced the cross. While Rasputin's back was to him, the prince slid open a drawer and gripped a Browning revolver. It was now or never. The prince fired and Rasputin wheeled around with a dazed expression and managed a roar of pain as he smashed to the floor. The prince was relieved and watched the monk slowly lose consciousness. Crouching over the fallen Rasputin, the prince gasped as Rasputin moved. In an instant the monk's hand tore at Yussupov's throat like a manacle. The prince shook loose and hurried for the stairs with Rasputin staggering after him. Both men screamed. One of the conspirators ran from the upper room and saw the bleeding Rasputin dragging himself from the house to the exit gate of the property. Chasing after the monk, he aimed his revolver at Rasputin, hitting him in the head with one of four shots. The other plotters arrived to see the monk collapse. Rasputin still was not dead. His eyes registered hatred and contempt for his attackers. Even as he moaned, they corraled him into a huge sack and bound it with a rope. Not far from the palace was the Neva Canal, and with a pitchfork, they penetrated the frozen deep, shoving the half-dead monk into the icy torrent. The body was recovered some days later and it was determined that Rasputin's death resulted from drowning. Born in Siberia, Russia, probably in 1871, he was forty-four years old.

NICHOLAS II

Last Monarch of Russia: Czar Nicholas II abdicated on March 15, 1917.

Background: Upon the abdication of Czar Nicholas II, the czar's brother, Grand Duke Michael, refused to take the throne unless through a free election. Due to the political upheaval overtaking Russia, a freely elected assembly could not be found, and hence the Russian monarchy in power since 1462 came to an end.

RUSSIAN REVOLUTION

Last Day: The last day of the Russian (or Bolshevik) Revolution was November 7, 1917 (October 25, old style calendar). On the night of November 6, Bolshevik leaders Nikolai Lenin and Leon Trotsky toppled the Provisional Government headed by Aleksandr Kerensky. Kerensky fled for his life, eventually escaping abroad. Lenin became Premier, Trotsky, became commissar for foreign affairs. The Provisional Government that had forced out the czar decided to continue Russia's participation in World War I, while many of its body represented the country's middle class.

Background: On March 3, 1861, Czar Alexander II of Russia abolished serfdom, thus transforming peasants into tenant farmers. Shortly thereafter the nobles of Russia demanded a constitution and a legislature. The czar at first balked at the nobles' demands but eventually relented, establishing a legislature on March 13, 1880, which was also the day the czar was assassinated. He was succeeded by his son, Alexander III, who was not party to the reforms granted by his father. Alexander III sought to turn back the clock. His efforts made him enemies, among them Alexander Ulyanov, who was implicated in a plot to murder the czar. When he was executed, his brother vowed vengeance and changed his name to Lenin.

Alexander III died on November 1, 1894, and Nicholas II became czar of Russia. He was not a strong-willed man; in fact he was too gentle. He had married the former Alexandra Feodorovna, beautiful granddaughter of Queen Victoria of Great Britain, a willful, domineering women who put her family before her country and thus inadvertently betrayed the Russian people. On August 4, 1904, a son named Alexis was born with hemophilia, and this caused the czar and czarina untold grief. But the czarina vowed to bring the child peace at all cost, for this child was destined to be the next czar of Russia. The czarina found her savior in a mystic named Grigory Rasputin who was the answer to her prayer, for he brought peace and healing to Alexis, if only for short periods. With time, the czarina would come to rely on Rasputin in affairs of state, to the detriment of the Russian people. A historian later wrote: "The nursery was the center of all Russia's troubles."

Though the birth of their only son after four daughters had brought some joy to the czar, it happened at a difficult time for him and his people, for Russia was involved in a costly war with Japan, the Russo-Japanese War (1904–1905). The war was costing the nation heavy military losses, corruption of public officials was widespread, and hunger was becoming a problem in many cities. When the local elected body, the Zemstvos, advised the czar to pass measures granting more privileges to the people, such as freedom of religion and speech, Nicholas refused, engendering protests. Thousands marched on January 22, 1905, in what became known as Bloody Sunday. Czarist soldiers, on orders from Nicholas, fired on the protesters and killed many as they approached the imperial Winter Palace. Bloody Sunday sparked riots throughout Russia that lasted for months, with schools, office buildings, government offices, and trains shutting down. A mutiny of sailors on the battleship *Potemkin* resulted in rampaging mobs committing violence along the coast of the Black Sea. To placate the people, the czar in March 1906 sanctioned the legislative body the Duma, which would allow free elections throughout Russia. At last Russia had taken a giant step forward toward democracy.

But fate was unkind to Czar Nicholas and his people. On June 28, 1914, Archduke Franz Ferdinand of Austria was assassinated by a Serbian terrorist in central Yugoslavia. Austria within a month declared war on Serbia for not having secured the safety of her prince. Russia, an ally of Serbia, declared war on Austria. Soon other countries came into the war that was to become World War I. Russia found herself fighting not only Austria but mighty Germany. She lost tens of thousands of soldiers in the first year of the war and the death toll eventually reached more than two million.

Nicholas had the extreme misfortune to have unwise

ministers and spies in his immediate cadre of military advisers. The war had also created two million Russian refugees. But perhaps what made Nicholas's situation most distressing was the poor military advice given the czar by his wife—advice fed her by the man with the hypnotic blue eyes, the monk Grigory Rasputin. Aside from attending her son, Tsarevich Alexis, Rasputin counseled the czarina on military affairs, advice she daily conveyed to her husband in the form of letters to the war front. The czarina also listened to Rasputin's opinions concerning the daily running of the government in her husband's absence—advice that was blamed for the food and fuel shortages that were hitting one city after another. The masses were becoming desperate.

The Russian Revolution was begun on March 8, 1917, when thousands stormed bakeries in Petrograd (formerly St. Petersburg), clamoring for bread. On March 11, czarist troops fired on the mobs of bread seekers, killing many. The revolution, without a leader, was a spontaneous reaction to the terrible conditions that had resulted from weak leadership. Rethinking its position, for many of the soldiers were former peasants, the army garrisoned at Petrograd, numbering over 190,000, joined the protests, with Czar Nicholas becoming the focus of their extreme discontent. The protesters now comprised soldiers, peasants, factory workers, and intellectuals. With the nation crumbling, clearly something had to be done. On March 14, 1917, with the czar at the battlefront, far away from Petrograd, a provisional government was installed, headed by Aleksandr Kerensky, a lawyer.

On March 15, 1917, at Pskov, Russia, Czar Nicholas resigned, writing, "May the Lord God keep Russia." Kerensky continued in the war with Germany and Austria, fearing that losing the war would result in conquest by Germany.

Germany had a plan. She sided with Lenin in an effort to upset the pro-allied Russian provisional government. In a sealed train, with protection through battle lines, Germany sent Lenin back to Russia on April 16. Lenin, Leon Trotsky, and Joseph Stalin promised the people "peace, bread, and freedom": peace appealed to the military, bread to the peasantry, and freedom to the factory workers. The message was gratefully accepted. Kerensky fought back, organizing a free election to be held later that year in November. But in what became known as the October Revolution, Lenin and his growing army of Bolsheviks on November 7 took control of key buildings in Petrograd, and had a battleship fire upon the Winter Palace, Kerensky's headquarters. Kerensky withdrew from the scene, fleeing abroad. The Russian Revolution of 1917 was over. World War I ended with the signing of the Brest-Litovsk Treaty, which ceded great parcels of land to Germany, some of which was returned when Germany was eventually defeated. Civil war followed in Russia from 1918 to 1921 as Lenin embarked on the creation of a socialist state, ending private ownership of factories and land by requiring them to be given over to communal ownership, and nationalizing banks. With Lenin, Trotsky, Stalin, and others, the Bolsheviks ruled. Political opponents of the ideals of a new Russian Communist state were brutally crushed, bringing the civil war to a close in 1921.

Today the czars are gone, and Lenin, Stalin, and Trotsky as well, and only now is Mother Russia recognizing the infamies committed by those she trusted, men and women who could not give them peace, bread, or freedom.

MANFRED VON RICHTHOFEN

Last Combat Flight: The last air battle of Baron Manfred von Richthofen took place on April 21, 1918.

Background: The German World War I aviator known as the Red Baron was in command of his fighting squadron, the Flying Circus, so named because of the vivid colors of their planes. As he was piloting his crimson Fokker triplane, engaging RAF Sopwith Camel planes over France, heavy ground fire from machine guns ended the aviator's life. When he was struck in the chest by a Vickers machine gun bullet, Richthofen's plane hurtled toward the Somme River, where it crashed and exploded. Known as the Bloody Red Baron and the Red Knight, Richthofen compiled a spectacular record of eighty air victories. His renowned Flying Circus replaced one-to-one military air tactics in favor of team unity. The baron was twenty-six years old when he died.

NICHOLAS II AND THE RUSSIAN ROYAL FAMILY

Last Day of Life: Nicholas II and his family were assassinated on July 16, 1918.

Background: The place was the railway town of Ekaterinburg in Siberia, in the Urals, now known as Sverdlovsk, some thousand miles from Moscow. In a cold, damp house with modest amounts of food and harsh treatment, the royal family had lived as prisoners for at least four months, not knowing what to expect, yet expecting the worst now that Nikolai Lenin was premier of Russia. The royal family consisted of Czar Nicholas II, the czarina, born Alexandra Feodorovna, and their children— daughters Olga, Tatiana, Marie, and Anastasia, and son Alexis. Their physician, a nurse, a cook, and a lady in waiting were with them.

On the night of July 16, 1918, the royal family and personnel were suddenly awakened at midnight by their Bolshevik guards. Hardly allowed to dress properly, they were simply told that loyalist soldiers sought to capture the town. Hurried to the basement of the house, the family was asked to wait for a moment. The czar sat on one of three chairs, the czarina and their son seated on either side of him. The children shivered in their night-clothes and began to cry. The man in charge and responsible for the czar, Yakov Yurovsky, was a cruel, crude individual, a Bolshevik radical consumed with hatred for the imperial family. He stood before the prisoners as their anxiety mounted. Several soldiers entered the room holding rifles and guns and Yurovsky announced that the family were to be executed. The czarina with a shocked sigh began to make the sign of the cross. Hardly had she crossed her heart when gunfire struck her husband Nicholas and her son. With the screams of death came more shots fired at the czarina, the other children, and their retainers. A terror-filled servant and one of the children, Anastasia, attempted to flee. The detail reloaded and pumped more rounds into the royal family and attendants.

When the screams and moans had stopped, the guards proceeded to stab the bodies with their bayonets until Yurovsky was satisfied that all were dead. The torn remains of the murdered bodies were scrupulously examined before being wrapped in sheets. Taken to an abandoned mine, the bodies were mutilated and burned, and the ashes were treated with benzine and sulfuric acid. The Russian people were officially informed of the death of the czar, but not of his wife and family, on July 19, 1918.

In 1920, a story broke from inside Germany that one of the czar's children had survived the massacre of the royal family. A woman named Anna Anderson claimed to be the czar's daughter Anastasia. It has never been verified, but the Anderson-Anastasia controversy still lingers, as do questions about the specifics of the massacre itself.

CHARLES I

Last of the Hapsburgs: The last Hapsburg ruler stepped down on November 11, 1918, as Charles I (also known as Karl I) withdrew from all executive duties after unsuccessful attempts to improve imperial rule in Hungary by guaranteeing a more democratic program.

Background: The Hapsburg House was influential in the politics of Germany, Austria, Switzerland, the Netherlands, and later Spain, for six hundred years. It was founded by Emperor Rudolph I in 1273. The last ruler of the Hapsburg Dynasty was Charles VI, who died on October 20, 1740, at age fifty-five. The enduring Hapsburg House began to crumble with the defeat of the Central Powers at the end of World War I. Its last figure of importance was Dr. Otto Hapsburg-Lothringer, eldest son of Charles I. The Hapsburgs had close ties to the Roman Catholic Church. The house was able to expand in power and influence through matrimony as its sons and daughters married into foreign royal houses, for example, the wedding of Maximilian to Mary of Burgundy gave the Austrian house the Low Countries of Holland and Belgium. The house was weakened by the Thirty Years War when the dynasty failed to gain the German states.

The emergence of Maria Theresa, daughter of Charles IV, in 1740 was a high point in the Hapsburg House. She was a natural leader and one of the most politically astute women ever to reign over a country. The shrewd Maria Theresa, Empress of Austria for thirty-five years, enhanced the strength of the dynasty and continued the tradition of securing valuable marriages to the nobles of other nations. But one tragedy upon the mighty house occurred with the arranged marriage of her daughter, Marie Antoinette to the Dauphin of France, the future King Louis XVI. Only a few years after Maria Theresa's death of old age in 1780, this daughter—who broke her mother's heart with her inability to conduct herself as a proper queen—was executed by the guillotine. With the death of Maria Theresa—she died seated in a chair as she recited the rosary—the last great Hapsburg was gone. Unlike many monarchs of her day, she was popular with her people. A patron of the arts, she encouraged Mozart, who as a child played a duet on the harpsichord with Marie Antoinette. She fed the poor of Austria, encouraged painters, and put in sixteen-hour days on behalf of Austria and world affairs.

The later years of the Hapsburg Dynasty were marked by tragedies. In 1888 Austria's crown prince, Archduke Rudolph, thirty-one years of age, committed suicide on January 30 after killing his mistress at Mayerling, Vienna. His twenty-five-year-old nephew, Archduke Franz Ferdinand became heir apparent to the throne of Austria. The beautiful Empress Elizabeth, on September 10, 1898, in Vienna, was surprised by assassin Luigi Luchenie as she walked from her hotel; the man plunged a knife once through her breast, and she died soon after. On June 28, 1914 assassin Gavrilo Princip burst from a crowd in Sarajevo in Yugoslavia, fatally shooting Archduke Franz Ferdinand and his wife, Sophie, in their royal carriage.

The Hapsburg Dynasty is remembered for its opulent dress at a time when classical music, painting, and the writing of literature flourished. The "Hapsburg lip," a protruding lower lip, was a physical feature of all the Hapsburgs.

WORLD WAR I

Last Day: The armistice ending World War I was signed at Compiègne, France, on November 11, 1918.

Background: Known as the Great War, World War I was sparked by the assassination of Archduke Ferdinand and his wife, Sophie, on June 28, 1914 by a Serbian terrorist, Gavrilo Princip, in central Yugoslavia. Within a month after the assassination, his nation, Austria, declared war on Serbia, who had failed to protect the royal guests. Other countries took sides in the conflict. Russia, a friend of Serbia, and France declared war on Austria-Hungary. Germany declared war on France and Russia. Great Britain, Italy, and France declared war on Germany, with Italy also declaring war on Austria. Germany, Austria-Hungary, and Bulgaria and Turkey lined up as the Central Powers, opposing the Allies, or Triple Entente, consisting of France, Russia, Great Britain, and eventually the United States.

The United States entered World War I on April 6, 1917, motivated by Germany's unrestricted submarine warfare, aimed to a great extent at the United States to prevent it from trading with the Allies, and by the sinking of the *Lusitania* on May 7, 1915. Among the 1,198 to perish were 128 Americans. The final straw was Germany's submarine sinking of the U.S.S. *Housatonic,* which caused the United States to sever diplomatic relations with Germany. These events resulted on April 6, 1917, in President Woodrow Wilson's request to Congress for a declaration of war against Germany. The supreme Allied commander was Marshal Foch, with General John J. Pershing as the commander-in-chief of the U.S. Expeditionary Forces.

Over eight million soldiers and civilians lost their lives. The peace treaty, the Treaty of Versailles, placed indemnities so severe on Germany—some $32 million in goods—that she became a vagabond nation and looked to an Austrian World War I veteran for leadership, one who promised to abrogate the Treaty of Versailles and restore Germany to her former greatness. His name was Adolf Hitler.

THEODORE ROOSEVELT

(Twenty-sixth President of the United States)

Last Day Of Life: Theodore Roosevelt died on January 6, 1919.

Background: The happy Teddy, who loved nature, still was good-humored in the last years of his life in spite of the loss of a son in World War I and his ill health, most humiliating of which was the loss of hearing in his left ear. He went home to Sagamore Hill near Oyster Bay, New York, at Christmastime in 1918 because he wanted to roam the woods of his childhood. Suffering from a flaring case of inflammatory rheumatism, on the night of January 5, 1919, he spoke his last words: "Please put out the lights." On January 6, at dawn, after breathing heavily, Theodore Roosevelt passed away. Born on October 27, 1858, in New York City, he was sixty years old. Death was caused by coronary embolism.

Gravesite: Young's Memorial Cemetery, Oyster Bay, New York.

FRIEDRICH WILHELM II

Last Monarch of Germany: Germany's Kaiser (Emperor) Friedrich Wilhelm II abdicated on November 28, 1919.

Background: Upon the collapse of the Second German Empire, Kaiser Friedrich Wilhelm II fled his nation to the Netherlands on November 10, 1918. He abdicated his throne on November 28, 1919. A republic was proclaimed at Weimar (hence Weimar Republic) with Friedrich Ebert as president. Germany's last monarch died in 1941.

WOODROW WILSON
(Twenty-eighth President of the United States)

Last Day in Office: March 4, 1921, after two terms.

Background: Woodrow Thomas Wilson's presidency was one of the most significant in American history. Though Wilson was up to the task, he was not the most physically strong of men. He was plagued with neuritis in his left leg and an old hernia also nagged him occasionally, causing great pain. Not being robust and prone to anxiety and worry by the end of his life, he felt relieved that his final moment was upon him. Wilson took office on March 4, 1913, and perhaps the most earth-shaking event at the outset of his presidency was Knute Rockne's use of the forward pass to bring victory for Notre Dame over Army the following autumn.

But Europe was about to explode. A First Balkan War was no sooner over when a Second Balkan War erupted. It was settled after a month's fight, and Europe enjoyed a fragile peace. In 1914 a Serbian assassinated Archduke Franz Ferdinand of Austria, resulting in Austria's declaration of war against Serbia. Within a month Europe was in turmoil. Wilson wanted no part of the European conflict, maintaining U.S. neutrality. The sinking of the *Lusitania* began to change public opinion about entering the war, but it was not enough to make Congress act. In the meantime Wilson concerned himself with Pancho Villa, the Mexican bandit, ordering General John J. Pershing to capture him dead or alive after Villa's forces killed seventeen Americans in New Mexico.

With the German sinking of the U.S.S. *Housatonic,* the United States broke off diplomatic relations with Germany on February 3, 1917, and on April 6, Wilson endured the first major setback of his presidency when he signed a joint Congressional resolution declaring the United States to be in a state of war with Germany. The president had broken a campaign promise to keep the United States neutral if reelected. The burden of sending Americans to war on foreign shores where many would die caused his health to weaken. Formulating Fourteen Points as a basis for peace with Germany, Wilson achieved an armistice, and for his efforts he won the Nobel Peace Prize. To ensure peace for all time the Versailles Conference adopted a resolution to establish a League of Nations Wilson had called for. When the U.S. Senate balked at passing the covenant for peace, Wilson attempted a nationwide tour of the United States, further weakening his health.

The president could look back on some fine domestic achievements, such as the passing of the Nineteenth Amendment giving women the right to vote, a Workman's Compensation Act, and a Federal Child Law, but the desire for a lasting peace through a League of Nations consumed Wilson's thoughts. The president suffered a stroke in October 1919 and became an invalid. Wilson ended his presidency without having realized his dream of a League of Nations. After leaving office, Wilson remained in Washington in retirement, writing and taking occasional spring walks with his wife, though he was obliged to depend on a cane—"my third leg," as he was fond of saying. His devoted wife, Edith, rarely left his side, and it was to her that he spoke his last words: "I'm ready," on February 1, 1924, two days before he died.

WARREN GAMALIEL HARDING
(Twenty-ninth President of the United States)

Last Day of Life: Warren G. Harding died on August 2, 1923, during his first term as president.

Background: The man who did not really have the heart for the job of president, preferring to remain a senator from Ohio, lived well as president. He ate too much and drank lots—even though he went on record as being in favor of Prohibition. With scandal after scandal plaguing his presidency, Harding had a stroke on a train while headed for Seattle. Taken to San Francisco, he was put to bed at the Palace Hotel. There the handsome president was expected to rest. However, believing himself to be well, he invited his wife—whom Harding called the Duchess—to read an article entitled "A Calm View of a Calm Man," which praised him and began to lift his morale. When his wife paused, Harding said his last words: "That's good. Go on, read some more." Suddenly falling to one side, Harding shook violently. His face pale and pained, Harding lifted himself up, only to collapse back on his pillow, dead. Born November 2, 1865, in Morrow, County, Ohio, he was fifty-seven years old.

Warren Harding's time in office was a long party. He gambled with his cronies, gave his friends jobs, and loved to attend baseball games and compete in marathon dances instead of attending to world affairs. If he was urgently needed, he could be found on the golf course, at some fancy restaurant, or in a gaming house. His wife nagged him, but his mistress, Nan Britton, made him remember his youth. Harding was not necessarily corrupt but was perhaps just too gullible to believe that his friends and appointees were.

Gravesite: Marion Cemetery, Marion, Ohio.

WOODROW WILSON
(Twenty-eighth President of the United States)

Last Day of Life: Woodrow Wilson died on February 3, 1924.

Background: By February 2, 1924, Woodrow Wilson had lost his power to speak and could recognize no one. An occasional incoherent whisper was all the life left in him. On February 3, with throngs keeping vigil outside his Washington home, Wilson's thin face became serene and his eyes radiant. As he held his wife's hand, all sense of life vanished from his eyes. Woodrow Wilson was dead. He was the last U.S. president elected without the women's vote. Born on December 28, 1856, in Staunton, Virginia, he was sixty-seven years old.

Gravesite: National Cathedral, Washington, D.C.

THE OTTOMAN DYNASTY

Last Ottoman Ruler: The last Ottoman ruler, Mohammed VI, fell on March 3, 1924, ending political power in Turkey that began with the capture of Constantinople in 1453.

Background: The reign of the Ottoman in the middle of the sixteenth century extended from the Persian Gulf to the borders of Poland, from the Caspian Sea to parts of Algeria. Having replaced the Seljuk Turks, the Ottoman, or Othman, Empire began in the thirteenth century with King Osman Al Ghazi, who had succeeded his father. For six centuries their power in the Mediterranean was absolute and had reunited the Islamic world from the Balkans to Tunis in North Africa. The dynasty's grip began to slip when its armies met a serious Arab uprising at Medina in June 1916. The beginning of the end came with the Turks having to defend the important strategic Dardanelles at the cost of Allied victories in Palestine, Syria, and Mesoptamia during World War I.

In 1920 Mustafa Kemal was elected president of Turkey and through diplomacy, the former war hero was able to get back the lands of Adrianople and Trace in exchange for neutralization of the Dardanelles. Kemal, who became Ataturk (meaning "Father of the Turks") in 1934 when he became dictator, took Turkey into the twentieth century, bringing an end to Muslim dress codes, declaring a republic, and abolishing the caliphate. The Ottoman House was banished from Turkey.

FORD TIN LIZZIE

Last Day Produced: On May 31, 1927, the Ford Motor Company produced its last Tin Lizzie.

Background: Ford began making the car in 1908, and it sold millions; when the Tin Lizzie died, it was selling for less than $400.

KNUTE ROCKNE

Last Defeat: Football coach Knute Rockne's last loss came when Notre Dame lost to Southern California, 27–14 on December 1 in the 1928 season. This season of five wins and four losses was the low point of a career that spanned the years 1918 to 1930.

Background: Born in Norway in 1888, Rockne coached Notre Dame in football for twelve years. Known as the Bald Eagle, he graduated in 1924 with a B.S. degree. As a football genius, he is remembered for the development of the precision backfield, and the then seldom used forward pass, which he popularized. But he is probably most remembered for his "Four Horsemen" players—Elmer Dayden, Harry Stuhldreher, Don Miller, and Jim Crowley—who made up the unstoppable Notre Dame backfield, ennobled to this day in college football annals for their speed and power. These four were supported by a Rockne "Seven Mule Line," shock troops that destroyed the opposition. When told of Knute Rockne's sudden death, Yale football coach Marvin A. Stevens said: "Rockne was the greatest of football teachers. His delightful sense of humor, his quick sympathy for the fallen adversary and his indomitable spirit are more than a legend and he will carry on as an inspiration to all who love the game of football."

ARNOLD ROTHSTEIN

Last Day of Life: Gambler Arnold Rothstein was shot to death on November 4, 1928.

Background: Gambler and businessman, suave and very wealthy, Rothstein was called A.R. Having left Lindy's Restaurant on November 4, 1928, to meet someone in Central Park, New York City, he was next seen staggering near the entrance of The Central Park Hotel with a bullet wound in the stomach. After he was taken to Polyclinic Hospital, his dying gesture was to put his finger to his lips to symbolize his un-

willingness to reveal who shot him. Within moments
A.R. was dead.

Worth millions from his gambling enterprises, he employed mobsters such as Legs Diamond to keep people
in line as he kept his speakeasies going. He was supposedly involved in the Black Sox baseball scandal, though
it was never proven. In the end, the forty-six-year-old
gambler failed to pay a quarter of a million dollars in a
card game debt, and his enemies dealt him a fatal hand
to even the score. He was born in New York City in 1882.

CALVIN COOLIDGE
(Thirtieth President of the United States)

Last Day in Office: March 4, 1929, after almost two terms.
Calvin Coolidge became the thirtieth president upon
the death of Warren G. Harding.

Background: Calvin Coolidge might be called the
greatest nonentity in history. He said very little and, as
president, did very little. Called Silent Cal, he is remembered for such ditties as: "The business of America is
business." "If you don't say anything you won't be called
on to repeat it." Coolidge did brighten up the White
House at Christmas in 1923 when he pulled the switch
on the first national outdoor Christmas tree. Coolidge
was president at a time when Americans watched with
fascination the Roaring Twenties, populated by gangsters like Al Capone and Arnold Rothstein, and sports
heroes like Babe Ruth and Knute Rockne. The Tin
Lizzie was putting middle-income Americans on the
road; flagpole sitters, speakeasies, and ladies with rolled
stockings were popular. In Hollywood the stars of the
day were Francis X. Bushman, Charlie Chaplin, and Rudolph Valentino; the aviation star was Charles A. Lind-
bergh. Through his term, Coolidge was a conservative,
nodded to big business, and followed a laissez-faire philosophy. His policies were kind to the stock market:
Speculation was supported by a president known for his
honesty and not his ingenuity.

AL CAPONE

Last Homicides: Al (Alphonse) Capone committed his last homicides on May 7, 1929, at a banquet he gave at the Hawthorn Hotel Cicero in Chicago. Having discovered a plot to kill him, Capone pounded three of his henchmen to death with a baseball bat. The victims were Albert Anselmi, John Scalise, and Joseph "Top Toad" Giunta.

Background: Born in Naples, Italy, in 1899, Capone was known as Scarface (a name he hated), having suffered a razor slash in a fight as a youth. As a young man Capone entered the employ of mobster Johnny Torrio, who with men like Capone sought to control Chicago bootleg operations. Capone committed numerous murders, but it was the murder of mobster Big Jim Colisimo on March 21, 1921, that made him famous. He is remembered as the brains behind the St. Valentine's Day Massacre, of February 14, 1929, a crime in which mobsters of a rival faction were machine-gunned to death in a Chicago garage. He headed the Chicago syndicate, a network of bootlegging, prostitution, gambling, slot machines, extortion, protection, blackmail, loan sharking and bribery, particularly of judges and politicians and police officials. When Capone faded from the crime scene, his shoes were filled by crime czar Charles "Lucky" Luciano of the syndicate known as Murder Incorporated.

KNUTE ROCKNE

Last Game: Football coach Knute Rockne's Fighting Irish of Notre Dame rolled over the University of Southern California 27–0 December 6, 1930. With the win over the USC Trojans, Rockne had compiled a perfect season of ten wins and no defeats, giving him a career record of 105 wins, twelve losses, and five ties.

WILLIAM HOWARD TAFT

(Twenty-seventh President of the United States)

Last Day of Life: William H. Taft died on March 8, 1930.

Background: President Taft, the Chief Justice of the Supreme Court since 1920, was suffering from high blood pressure and was unable to take nourishment. He had barely been able to add his signature to a Supreme Court document. On March 8, 1930, while sleeping, he had a heart attack and never regained consciousness before he died. Born on September 15, 1857, in Cleveland, Ohio, he was seventy-two years old.

Gravesite: Arlington National Cemetery, Arlington, Virginia.

JUDGE CRATER

Last Seen: On August 6, 1930, Judge Crater waved goodbye from a taxi moving west on Forty-fifth Street in New York City.

Background: Judge Joseph Force Crater, a New York State Supreme Court judge, dressed in a dark brown, double-breasted suit with green stripes and wearing a Panama hat, was on his way to the David Belasco Theatre to attend the last act of the play *Dancing Partner.* The last known persons to see the Judge were a lawyer named William Klein and a showgirl named Sally Lou Ritz. The disappearance of Judge Crater is the most famous of disappearances in the annals of missing persons and quite fascinating, for it came to light in a big way—on the front page of the powerful old *New York World* on September 1, 1930. On that day File 13595 of the New York Missing Persons Bureau was born.

The last known day of the forty-two-year-old Crater's life was hectic—a day on which he seemed to be racing against time to meet some deadline. In his New York law office at 11 A.M., he had his secretary, Joseph L. Mara, running to banks to cash checks of $3,000 and $2,150. In the meantime, Crater was busy trying to stuff folders into a too-small briefcase—until he called for a larger case of satchel size. When the money was brought from the bank, Crater carelessly shoved it into his inside suit-jacket pocket, and then proceeded to clear his office of personnel. A visitor, Simon F. Rifkind, paid the judge a call, and after his departure, Crater and his secretary took a taxi to Crater's Fifth Avenue apartment with the documents. Excusing Mara, his last words to the man were: "I'm going up to Westchester Way for a swim."

Judge Crater was next seen that evening in the Broadway district where he inquired at a ticket agency for a ticket to the play *Dancing Partner* at the David Belasco Theatre. Afterward he attended a dinner engagement at Hass' Restaurant on Forty-fifth Street and Broadway. He seemed to be in a cordial if not jovial mood.

An important judge, appointed by the then Governor Franklin Roosevelt, Crater was greeted by many of the patrons before dining with lawyer William Klein and Sally Lou Ritz. At 9:15 P.M. he hailed the taxi that Klein and Ritz thought would take him only a few blocks away to the Belasco Theatre. Judge Crater after stepping into that taxi was never seen again. According to File 13595, a ticket in Crater's name was picked up at the theater and Crater is believed to have attended the performance. When last seen, Crater was not overburdened with papers, which led some to theorize that he had concluded his business that afternoon. This business was, to say the least, of a secretive nature.

The first episode of the Crater case had begun when Crater was at his Maine vacation retreat with his wife, Stella. On August 3 the telephone rang. Slamming the phone down after speaking, Crater told his wife he was going to New York. He did not disclose the name of the caller. He did say, "I've got to straighten those fellows out . . ." He promised to be back within a week—in time for his wife's birthday.

The news of Judge Crater's disappearance became an international event—an event that to this day baffles criminologists. There were many theories, one more fascinating than the other. A popular one is that the judge was involved with various women and was killed in a blackmail scheme. Another theory concerns corruption: An envelope found by Crater's wife after his disappearance contained checks, cash, and instructions to make good on certain outstanding loans with the funds. She was also instructed that the envelope was to be kept confidential. At the end of his instructions were written: "I am very weary. Love Joe."

On June 6, 1939, almost nine years after Judge Joseph Force Crater disappeared and more than half a million dollars had been spent trying to locate him, he was legally declared dead. Police from New York have followed up clues from around the world, but nothing concerning Crater's whereabouts was ever substantiated. File 13595 is today a bulging mass of papers, filling several drawers, with new information occasionally being added. The best detectives have tried to solve the puzzle, but the fate of the judge seems destined to remain a mystery forever.

THOMAS EDISON

Last Patented Invention: Edison applied for a patent for a phonograph needle in 1931, last year of the inventor's life. The needle improved the quality of the phonograph machine Edison invented back in 1878, not as a means for reproducing music, but as a way of recording the spoken word.

Last Experiment: Edison's last experiment was on specimens from the goldenrod plant in an effort to produce rubber. It was not successful.

KNUTE ROCKNE

Last Day of Life: Football coach Knute Rockne was killed in a plane crash in Bazaar, Kansas, on April 1, 1931, at age forty-three.

AL CAPONE

Last Conviction: Al Capone received a sentence of eleven years at Leavenworth Prison, Kansas, and was fined $50,000 for tax evasion, plus $30,000 in court costs, on November 24, 1931.

LEGS DIAMOND

Last Crime: Diamond seriously injured Grover Parks, a bootlegger, and kidnapped bartender James Duncan on December 11, 1931—crimes for which he was acquitted.

Last Day of Life: Legs Diamond was murdered on December 18, 1931.

Background: Legs Diamond was happy on his last day of life, and after celebrating at a Troy, New York, saloon and spending time with his girlfriend, he went home to his Albany rooming house. He was asleep in his room on December 18, 1931, when hired gunmen shot him to death. It is not clear what exactly happened, but five shots rang out, awakening the landlady. Police were summoned and discovered that the man who claimed he couldn't be killed was dead. Five steel-jacketed bullets had pierced his head and lower body. He was thirty-five years old.

Born John Thomas Diamond in Philadelphia, Pennsylvania, in 1896, Legs began his crime life as a child. His ability to swipe packages from mail trucks and flee with ease earned him the nickname Legs. His exploits consisted of murder, narcotics trafficking, extortion, hijacking, and prostitution. He was able to thrive thanks to a lenient justice system. It was never proven, but he was reputed to have been in the employ of Dutch Schultz.

CLARENCE DARROW

Last Case: The Tommy Massie case was the eloquent defense attorney's last. On April 5, 1932, his client was found guilty.

Background: Tommy Massie was convicted of killing a Hawaiian athlete, believing that the man was part of a gang that raped his wife, Thalia Massie. The murdered athlete was innocent, and though a Hawaiian court found Massie and cohorts guilty of manslaughter, the great American criminal lawyer's argument obtained their freedom after only one hour in the sheriff's custody. Famous Darrow cases, included the Scopes Monkey Trial and the Leopold-Loeb case. Clarence Darrow died on March 13, 1938, at age eighty-one.

PRETTY BOY FLOYD

Last Confirmed Homicide: Floyd's last hit took place on April 7, 1932, when he shot Erv A. Kelley, a special investigator of Oklahoma, as Floyd escaped from a police dragnet.

Background Floyd was hailed by the farmers in the midwestern and southwestern regions as a Robin Hood of sorts. Floyd claimed to have only stolen from "moneyed men." Farmers in debt to the banks Floyd robbed were able to pay off their debts thanks to Floyd's generosity.

MAD DOG COLL

Last Homicide: In mid-July, 1932, Mad Dog Coll, in an attempt to machine-gun rival gangsters, scattered a play street with gunfire, killing five-year old Michael Vengalli instead, while wounding several other children.

Last Day of Life: Mad Dog Coll was murdered in late 1932.

Background: Some question as to the exact date of Mad Dog Coll's death exists, but it was in late 1932. Coll had a price on his head of $50,000, put there by Dutch Schultz for, among other things, killing one of Schultz's lieutenants and the man's girl friend. Married just four days, the twenty-four-year-old Coll was making a telephone call on West Twenty-Third Street in New York when the phone booth exploded from a hit man's machine gunfire, killing Coll instantly. He was born Vincent Coll in New York City in 1909.

Coll got his name Mad Dog after his rampant shooting spree that resulted in the death of his last victim. He was a hated killer, almost fearless. His crimes consisted of coldblooded murders, extortion, kidnapping, bootlegging, and grand larceny. As a child, he was orphaned and eventually went to reform school. The well-established mobsters like Dutch Schultz and Lucky Luciano were uneasy with him because they believed he was a crazy young man who couldn't be bargained with.

HERBERT CLARK HOOVER
(Thirty-first President of the United States)

Last Day in Office: March 4, 1933, after one term.

Background: Hoover was in office as president for some seven months when on Tuesday, October 29, 1929—Black Tuesday—the stock market collapsed. The entertainment newspaper *Variety* minced no words with its historic headline: "Wall St. Lays an Egg." Thousands of investors were wiped out and a period of unparalleled economic depression gripped the world. Line-ups became the scene everywhere throughout the United States: citizens lining up to withdraw their savings from banks; unemployed workers lining up for bread and soup; job-seekers lining up for contracts to sell apples; homeowners and farmers lining up with guns, pitchforks, and knives to welcome tax and bank interests seeking to confiscate property; the homeless lining up for shelter from the cold and elements. Hoover would not dole out government money to the unemployed, telling the puzzled masses that the nation had turned the corner on its economic woes. America's thirty-first president refused to believe that the economy was in a state of desperation, with its citizens sorrowing and despairing.

Then on a hot July night in 1932, ten thousand veterans marched on the Capitol. The out-of-work veterans who had been promised a bonus of $1,000 apiece—not due to them for twenty years—demanded the money at once. News of a no vote in the Senate spread over the Capitol steps down to the grounds, and within minutes pushing exploded into panic and eventually a riot. But even that was eventually smothered in a spirit of patriotism as the veterans, who came to be known as the Bonus Boys, sang "My Country 'Tis of Thee." Hoover was not happy at the sight of the ragged ex-soldiers slumming on the Capitol mall. He unleashed the army upon them—soldiers under the command of General Douglas MacArthur and Major Dwight Eisenhower. With tear gas, cocked rifles with bayonets, and clubs they cleared the Capitol grounds.

Hoover got the job done and turned American hearts against him. At the time the Democrats were holding their convention in Chicago and used the issue as one reason for turning out Hoover and seeking a "New Deal" with Franklin D. Roosevelt.

In fairness to Hoover, the nation's economic woes did not begin overnight. When he took office big business dominated the Federal Trade Commission, which became a rubber stamp for the corporations of America. Before the stock market crash, margin requirements for purchasing stocks and securities were too low and unregulated, which only encourage speculation. Hoover, a Republican, was also without the benefit of a Republican majority in Congress. He was soundly defeated in his bid for reelection in 1932. In later years he was devoted to government service, helping in programs to aid postwar Europe. In 1947 and again in 1953 he headed a commission responsible for recommendations to improve government on all levels; it now bears his name.

GOLD DOLLAR

Last Time Gold Dollar Was U.S. Currency Standard: April 4, 1933, was the last day of the gold standard. The next day, by presidential order, Americans were obliged to turn in their gold coins and gold certificates to banks for conversion to silver dollars.

Background: The gold dollar had become part of the U.S. currency standard back in 1873, with the $10 and $20 gold pieces becoming popular.

CALVIN COOLIDGE
(Thirtieth President of the United States)

Last Day of Life: Calvin Coolidge died on June 5, 1933.

Background: At his home in Northampton, Massachu-setts, the former president went to his kitchen for a glass of water after trying his hand at a puzzle in his library. Afterward he looked in on a servant in his basement to observe the furnace being stoked. It was still morning on June 5, 1933, and Coolidge was in the mood for a morning nap. When his wife went to awaken him for a light lunch, she discovered her husband dead of a heart attack on the bedroom floor. Born July 4, 1872, in Plym-outh, Vermont, he was sixty years old. He was famous for saying, "I do not choose to run."

Gravesite: Notch Cemetery, Plymouth, Vermont.

PRETTY BOY FLOYD

Last Persons Killed: The Kansas City Massacre, in which an FBI agent, four other law officers, and their charge, a criminal named Frank Nash, died in a hail of machine-gun fire, occured on June 17, 1933. According to Floyd, he was not the machine-gun killer, but law officers placed him at the scene and thought he was indeed the killer.

PROHIBITION

Last Day: On December 5, 1933, the Twenty-first Amend-ment to the United States Constitution took effect, re-pealing the Eighteenth Amendment, thus making the manufacture and sale of alcoholic beverages again legal in the United States.

Background: The manufacture, transportation, and sale of alcoholic beverages had been suspended thirteen years before with the Volstead Act (after Congressman Andrew Volstead, its sponsor) and Eighteenth Amend-ment to the U.S. Constitution, on January 16, 1920.

Looking back on the period known as Prohibition, historians agree that the ban on alcoholic beverages was not worthwhile, for it gave rise to bootlegging and gangster warfare by such men as Al Capone and Dutch Schultz. They headed crime organizations that raked in millions, spilling much blood in their wake.

Prohibition added new words to the American vocabulary. *Bootleg:* a smuggler of whiskey who concealed a bottle in the leg of a high boot, and the act of illegal sale of alcoholic beverages. *Bathtub gin:* a cheap alcoholic mix of gin and ginger ales or orange juice prepared in a tub. *Blind pig:* an unlicensed liquor establishment. *Home brew:* illegal alcoholic beverages prepared at home, very often in the basement. *Jake:* an alcoholic beverage made from Jamaica ginger. *Speakeasy:* a club serving illegal beverages where admittance was gained by flashing an identification card through a door peephole.

JOHN DILLINGER

Last Murder Charge: Dillinger was fingered by police for the machine-gun slaying of policeman Patrick O'Malley on January 15, 1934, when O'Malley attempted to intervene in the robbery of the First National Bank in East Chicago, Indiana.

Background: Like Bonnie and Clyde and Baby Face Nelson, Dillinger participated in bank robberies and was reputed to have committed murders. He once escaped prison by fashioning a handmade gun made out of soap. The handsome Dillinger had no trouble finding ladies, one of whom betrayed him in the end. Hollywood films have romanticized his life.

Last Confirmed Bank Robbery: John Dillinger's last robbery took place in Mason City, Iowa, on March 13, 1934, when in the company of Baby Face Nelson, Homer Van Meter, Tommy Carrol, and Hamilton Green, Dillinger held up the First National City Bank for $52,000, far short of the $200,000 they expected. The police apparently had been alerted. Taking hostages, the robbers escaped by the skin of their teeth with police holding their fire to save the lives of the many hostages. The twenty innocent bystanders were set free unharmed.

BONNIE AND CLYDE

Last Homicide: Having a picnic in a field near Grapevine, Texas, on April 1, 1934, Bonnie and Clyde spotted two state troopers approaching them. Before words could be exchanged, Bonnie and Clyde shot the officers to death.

Last Day of Life: Bonnie and Clyde were killed on May 23, 1934.

Background: Six officers (Texas Rangers and county officers) waited on top of a little hill alongside a road near Gibsland, Louisiana, on May 23, 1934. They spotted Bonnie and Clyde's small sedan and hollered out to them to surrender. Clyde went for his gun, but before he could fire a shot, the officers opened fire, stitching 167 bullets into the car, fifty killing Bonnie and Clyde. As the officers approached the car, the outlaws were both sitting in the front seat, Clyde holding his gun in his hand, Bonnie with her head between her knees, a machine gun across her lap. She was clutching a package of bloodsoaked cigarettes in her left hand. The fingers of her right hand that had gripped the trigger were shot away.

Bonnie Parker and Clyde Barrow, contrary to Hollywood's glamorous image, were actually sadistic killers. The pair once pulled up to a traffic officer to ask directions and thanked the man by killing him with a shotgun blast. The idea that they were Robin Hoods is a myth. They were self-indulgent and stingy, specializing in bank, grocery store, and gas station robberies. They were bloodletters in the true sense of the word.

JOHN DILLINGER

Last Alleged Bank Robbery: The Merchant National Bank in South Bend, Indiana, was robbed of $18,000 on June 30, 1934. Dillinger was placed at the scene of the crime by local police, though his presence was unconfirmed by the FBI.

Last Day of Life: John Dillinger was killed on July 22, 1934.

Background: With a $10,000 reward on his head—dead or alive—on the steamy night of July 22, 1934, in Chicago, Illinois, Dillinger was on his way to a movie at the Biograph Theatre with Anna Sage, the Woman in Red (though her dress was actually orange). Anna Sage was his lover, but she was about to betray him in a deal with the FBI. Approaching the movie house, Dillinger heard a voice say, "Hello John" as his two lady companions withdrew from his side. Alerted, Dillinger took off down an alley of the theater, but a hail of gunfire from FBI agents' guns blew him to the pavement. He was pronounced dead, bringing to a close a desperate life. Born in Indianapolis, Indiana, in 1902, he was thirty-two years old.

MAURETANIA

Last Voyage: The graceful *Mauretania* made her final journey from New York to Southampton, England, on September 26, 1934.

Background: Grand lady of the sea, of classic beauty, with six decks and four funnels, with graceful sweep from stem to stern, the *Mauretania* won the prestigious sea prize, the Blue Ribbon for speed, unseating her sister ship, the ill-fated *Lusitania,* as the fastest luxury vessel. Built in 1907, she bade farewell to the sea on July 2, 1935 as she sailed to a Scotland scrapyard, having never suffered a blemish. Her speed was a nifty 25.5 knots.

BABE RUTH

Last Season with New York Yankees: Ruth left the Yankees after the 1934 season.

Background: Born George Herman Ruth in Baltimore, Maryland, on February 6, 1895, a child of the streets, Ruth by the age of ten was at St. Mary's Industrial School, where school officials hoped he would learn a trade. Put on the baseball team, Ruth became accomplished as a pitcher. Soon it became clear to Brother Albert, the coach, that Ruth had great potential as a baseball player. On his eighteenth birthday Ruth signed a contract with the old Baltimore Orioles. Eventually his contract was purchased from the Baltimore farm club by the Boston Red Sox.

His fame in the big leagues grew first as a pitcher and then as a hitter. Ruth was a portly six footer with a hilarious sense of humor. His fame spread and peaked with the Yankees, where he played and feuded with Lou Gehrig and drove manager Miller Huggins and owner Jacob Ruppert crazy with his weight problems, his humor, and his laxity when it came to curfews.

Ruth was flamboyant, crude, gentle, and a sucker for kids. He was one of the few ball players who gave children baseballs at games and pocket money for ice cream on the street, and he visited their sick brothers and sisters in hospitals. He had a temper and once charged a loudmouth fan in the stands behind home plate for annoying him. Ruth also had a fierce appetite, and it was common for him to polish off ten stadium hot dogs at one sitting.

PRETTY BOY FLOYD

Last Day of Life: On October 22, 1934, as Pretty Boy Floyd fled across an open field in Liverpool, Ohio, FBI gunfire brought him down. His last words were: "You've got me this time." Born in Akins, Oklahoma in 1901, he was thirty-three years old when he died.

BABY FACE NELSON

Last Killings and Last Day of Life: The day was November 27, 1934, on a country road outside Barrington, Illinois, when Baby Face Nelson brought his car to a sudden stop. He was being chased by FBI agents. Jumping from the car with a Thompson machine gun, he took on the two agents, Herman Hollis and Sam Cowley. Hollis and Cowley both died of machine gun fire. They succeeded in seriously wounding Nelson, whose dead body was discovered in a ditch near Niles, Illinois on November 28. He was twenty-six years old.

Background: Born Lester Gillis in Chicago in 1908, Nelson was small not only in physical stature but in mind as well. Little things upset him and he was known to work over his lady friends. He was employed by Al Capone to keep merchants in line and to beat up tardy payers for Capone protection. He hated the name Baby Face. The only thing he loved more than himself was his Thompson machine gun. It is not known how many people he killed, but his carelessness and his killing of FBI agents made him very dangerous to his mob friends.

BABE RUTH

Last Career Home Run: Ruth hit a center field shot off Pittsburgh Pirate pitcher Guy Bush at old Forbes Field in Pittsburgh on May 25, 1935, giving the Babe a total of 714 home runs. It was a memorable day because the home run king had previously hit two homers in the game for a total of three round trippers for the day.

Last at Bat in Regulation Game: On May 30, 1935, in Philadelphia, in a game against the Phillies, Babe Ruth, with the Boston Braves, hit a ground ball to the first baseman, Dolf Camilli. The Babe, forty-one years old, overweight, and tired, never played baseball in regulation season play again. He closed his baseball career with a dismal .181 batting average for the season.

Last Day of Baseball Career: On June 2, 1935, Babe Ruth was given his unconditional release by Boston Braves owner, Emil B. Fuchs, for violating the team curfew after the baseball star attended a shipboard party.

DUTCH SCHULTZ

Last Day of Life: Gangster Dutch Schultz was murdered on October 23, 1935.

Background: Schultz was being investigated by special prosecutor Thomas E. Dewey (later New York governor and presidential candidate) in an effort to curb New York racketeering. Schultz, called the Dutchman, decided to kill Dewey, and when the more level-headed factions of the mob, notably Lucky Luciano, would not give him the green light, he decided to disregard their advice, so he had to be stopped. On October 23, 1935, at the Palace Chop House in Newark, New Jersey, mob orders were about to be carried out—orders from the very top, Lepke Buchalter of the infamous Murder Incorporated. About 5 o'clock, Charlie "The Bug" Workman entered the Chop House and headed for the back of the restaurant where Schultz hung out. At a table sat two of Schultz's henchmen, Abe Landau and Otto "Aba Daba" Berman. Both men fell dead from a succession of .45-caliber bullets fired by Workman. Looking over the scene, Workman noticed the men's room and decided to check it out. In the washroom he saw a heavyset man washing his hands, and without asking the man's name, apparently familiar with Schultz's identity, he pumped two bullets into his stomach. After being taken to the hospital and after lengthy deathbed mutterings, Dutch Schultz died at 6:40 P.M. Born Arthur Flegenheimer in New York City in 1902, he was thirty-three years old.

Dutch Schultz graduated from petty crimes of his youth to become a highly successful bootlegger. He ordered other mobsters killed for getting in his way, including Mad Dog Coll and Legs Diamond.

CHARLES "LUCKY" LUCIANO

Last Crime: With other board members of the syndicate, Luciano ordered the murder of Dutch Schultz (two of Schultz's men were also killed) in a Newark, New Jersey restaurant on October 23, 1935. Charles Workman and Mendy Weiss were the hitmen. Actually Weiss did not enter the restaurant. He waited outside.

Background: Infamous Charles "Lucky" Luciano's life of crime began before he was ten years of age, when he engaged in shoplifting sprees and narcotics peddling.

Before he reached his twentieth birthday, he had committed several murders in New York City gang wars. He was arrested numerous times for his misdeeds. While in the employ of Jack "Legs" Diamond, Luciano is believed to have been the trigger man in the demise of gambler Arnold Rothstein. In 1929 he was made mafia chief of lower Manhattan rackets, having survived an attempt on his life only months before. In 1934, having ordered many murders, including those of rival gang bosses Salvatore Mauro and Silva Tagliagamba, Luciano consolidated his power. In league with mobsters Meyer Lansky, Louis "Lepke" Buchalter, Dutch Schultz, Albert Anastasia, and other notorious crime figures, he established a crime syndicate that would control brothels, narcotics, and contract murders by specially trained killers; this syndicate eventually turned on some of its own, among them, Dutch Schultz and Bugsy Siegel, both murdered at the behest of Luciano.

Luciano was slippery, never once being actually fingered in murder; his hired killers permanently silenced those who threatened to talk. However, he eventually tripped up when the enterprising New York prosecutor Thomas Dewey began looking into Luciano's activities and branded him Public Enemy Number One.

Pressure on New York City police caused Luciano to become their top priority. Madams and prostitutes started giving information on Lucky, and eventually he was nailed, convicted and sentenced to a long prison term. Having been influential in helping the navy with its security for the New York docks during World War II, Luciano, after numerous requests for parole, won his freedom with Meyer Lansky's help. A vastly wealthy man, he retired to Italy after several attempts to relocate in the United States; Luciano did manage to get to Cuba for a brief stay.

Last Conviction: Arrested in Hot Springs, Arkansas, in 1936, Luciano was returned to New York, where a grand jury indicted him on ninety counts of extortion and prostitution. Bail was set at $350,000. Lucky Luciano was convicted and sentenced to serve time at the Clinton state prison at Dannemora, New York for the term of thirty to fifty years. He was paroled in late 1945.

HINDENBURG

Last Day: The 803-foot zeppelin, the pride of Germany, crashed on the evening of May 6, 1937.

Background: At 7:25 P.M. as the *Hindenburg* began a descending pattern over Lakehurst, New Jersey, it exploded with the force of a powerful bomb blast, spilling liquid sheets of fire on some seven hundred sailors and technicians waiting below to assist the *Hindenburg* in its mooring. Thirty-six passengers out of ninety-seven lost their lives. Associated Press photographer Murray Becker caught the spectacular catastrophe, while reporter Herb Morrison's radio broadcast of the event became famous for his unabashed emotional expression of horror because it was the first broadcast to be recorded.

The *Hindenburg* had departed on May 3 from Frankfurt Aerodrome in Germany on its transatlantic voyage. To this day, the cause of the accident is not known, though Nazi sabotage or an electrical spark have been suspected as reasons for the demise of what turned out to be the last passenger airship and the end of future zeppelin dreams. Germany withdrew the *Hindenburg*'s sister ship, the *Graf Zeppelin,* from service. The airship was named after the German general and president Paul von Hindenburg (1847–1934).

AMELIA EARHART

Last Contact: Amelia Earhart was last heard from at 8:45 A.M., New York time, on July 2, 1937.

Background: With anxiety mounting on the Coast Guard cutter *Itasca,* stationed at Howland Island in the Pacific Ocean, a distant voice fighting static was suddenly heard making radio contact—a voice marked by fear and desperation. "We are in line position 157–337 . . . will repeat this message. We will repeat this message at 6210 kilocycles . . . Wait: Listening on 6210 kilocycles. We are running north and south.'' The message ended there. Never again would Amelia Earhart, age forty, known as A.E. by close friends, be heard from again.

The bright-faced, boyish-looking aviator was completing a last sweep in a round-the-world flight. Her last position was fixed somewhere between Australia and Howland Island. Her navigator was Fred L. Noonan, age forty-four. Earhart was last seen embarking on her last venture at an airstrip on Lae Island, New Guinea, on July 2, where she posed for pictures with her publisher husband George Putnam. At 10:30 A.M. (local time), July 2, 1937, her plane, the *Electra,* shot eastward ascending toward the overcast heavens. Her letters were KHAQQ.

Many theories abound as to the fate of Amelia Earhart and Fred Noonan, including speculation that they were on a spy mission, that they landed on Saipan Island and were executed by the Japanese, or that they ran out of fuel and crashed into the sea. Before the fateful flight, Amelia Earhart confided in her husband, ''Please know I am quite aware of the hazards. I want to do it—because I want to do it. Women must try to do things as men have tried. When they fail, their failure must be but a challenge to others.'' She promised her husband it was to be her last flight: ''Absolutely, the last one.''

BERENGARIA

Last Voyage: The *Berengaria* in March 1938 sailed from New York to Cherbourg, France, and Southhampton, England.

Background: Built in 1912 by Germany as a merchant vessel, the *Berengaria* was first named the *Imperator.* After World War I she fell into British hands, was sold to the Cunard line, and was converted to passenger service, renamed the *Berengaria.* In 1929, with hard times upon the world, the *Berengaria* became a cut-rate ocean liner, nicknamed the Bargain-area. A series of fires in her bulkheads due to faulty wiring made her a risk for underwriters and spelled her demise.

SPANISH CIVIL WAR

Last Day: On March 28, 1939, General Francisco Franco's Nationalists defeated the Loyalist Republicans.

Background: The Spanish Civil War began in 1936, but the seeds were planted in 1931 when Spain's Loyalists forced Alfonso XIII to leave the country on July 14, 1931, after municipal elections favored a republican form of government. In 1936 Francisco Franco, supported by the military, the aristocracy, the Church, and the monarchy—as well as by Hitler and Mussolini—engineered revolts in Madrid that later spread to other Spanish cities, including Seville, Burgos, and Cadiz. The Loyalists received meager support from Russia.

The bombing of Guernica, the Basque city in northern Spain, by German bombers on April 26, 1937, killed thousands—mainly victims of falling buildings. The destruction became the subject of a mural by Picasso. By March 1939 the death toll had reached the million mark. At war's end, Spain was in ruins. While Franco became dictator of Spain, he was unable to offer Germany or Italy support as Hitler prepared to invade Poland to start World War II. The death of General Francisco Franco on November 20, 1975, brought King Juan Carlos to the leadership of Spain.

NORMANDIE

Last Voyage: The *Normandie* sailed on August 28, 1939, from Le Havre, France, and Southampton, England, to New York.

Background: On a bitter cold day in February, 1942, tragedy struck the $6 million luxury liner *Normandie* when a workman's torch ignited a pile of mattresses. The ship was being prepared for troop service. Within an hour, a fantastic fire, fanned by freezing winds, engulfed the entire vessel, threatening piers as well. Many fire boats including those of the New York City Fire Department managed to put the fire out, but the *Normandie* was wa-

ter-logged, and with the severe cold, she became a frozen, gutted mass. She died at the scrapyards. Her
maiden voyage had been in 1936.

AL CAPONE

Last Day in Prison: On November 16, 1939, Al Capone was
released at midday from Alcatraz Prison, San Francisco,
California, for good behavior, with three years left to his
sentence for tax evasion.

BUGSY SIEGEL

Last Crime: Siegel murdered fellow gangster Whitney Krakower on a Brooklyn, New York, street, shooting him to
death on July 31, 1940, after Krakower had threatened
to talk to the police concerning a previous murder he
had committed with Siegel.

Background: In the annals of crime, few were
smoother, handsomer, or more ruthless and vicious
than Bugsy Siegel. (Bugsy was a name he hated.) In
his youth he set merchants' pushcarts on fire on the
lower East Side of New York if they failed to pay protection. With stunning blue eyes and curly hair, Siegel
could have become a Hollywood actor had he not
preferred the life of a gangster. He committed numerous murders, some in the employ of mobster
Meyer Lansky. One of Siegel's most brutal murders
occurred near the Brooklyn docks; on a hot October
night Siegel not only shot but stabbed his boyhood
friend, mobster Abe "Bo" Weinberg, and dumped his
body into the East River. No one knows how many
murders Siegel committed for Lansky, but he was also
involved in loansharking and blackmail.

When the police began closing in on him, his
bosses sent him out West. He eventually used mob
money to build the Flamingo Hotel, Las Vegas's first
gambling casino, in 1945, and thus transformed a
sleepy cow town into the gambling mecca of the
United States. Along the way he rubbed shoulders

with the famous, including George Raft, Clark Gable, and Jack Warner. He used beautiful women to satisfy his ravenous sexual appetite. Among them was the beautiful Virginia Hill. Their torrid affair was well-known in spite of the fact that Siegel was a married man with children. Some historians believe that Virginia Hill set him up for his murder, when she was conveniently absent the evening of his death at her mansion. In the eyes of his cohorts, Siegel had become too big for his britches. The most powerful man in mob history, Charles "Lucky" Luciano, to whom Siegel owed more than $5 million, had him erased.

LEON TROTSKY

Last Day of Life: Trotsky was assassinated on August 21, 1940.

Background: With Lenin, Trotsky was one of the leaders of the Russian Revolution that eventually established the USSR. Trotsky was a fiery intellectual who articulated the concept of pure Communism. In 1929, after years of feuding with Joseph Stalin, who was part of the governing triumvirate along with Lev Kamenev and Grigori Zinoviev, Trotsky was expelled. Moving around the world, having lived in Turkey, France, and Norway, Trotsky settled in Avenida Viena, Mexico, in a quaint and well-guarded residence, since he was quite aware that he was a marked man after publishing such works as *The Revolution Betrayed* and *The Stalin School of Falsification*. A commando squad of Russian agents armed with machine guns had made one attempt on his life in 1940. Stalin had already hatched another plan for dispatching Trotsky, who was undermining Stalin's socialist view of Communism.

An affable young man named Frank Jacson was romantically involved with one of Trotsky's secretaries, Sylvia Agelof. The situation looked innocent enough, though a security check of the man might have been warranted because of the way he spelled his last name, usually seen as Jackson. It later turned out that Jacson had a French passport listing his name as Jacques Mornard, while his birth certificate listed him as Spanish-born Ramon Mercader. Jacson had endeared himself to the Trotskys and their household, often being invited to the residence, and before long he and Trotsky were sharing ideas. One evening, August 20, 1940, Jacson showed up at the Trotsky residence wearing a coat, which no one found odd. Expressing a desire to enjoy the company of the old Bolshevik, Jacson was allowed to join Trotsky in his study, where it was thought he would seek advice concerning an article he had written on Communism. As Trotsky was reading the article, Jacson nervously moved behind him. Hovering over Trotsky, he slipped a small ax from his coat and smashed the tool into the old man's head. The blow drew a piercing cry from Trotsky, who, though seriously wounded, rose from his seat and engaged his attacker, biting Jacson's fingers. The two scuffled over a dagger that Jacson was trying to pull from his coat. Guards alerted by Trotsky's wife, Natalia, rushed into the study and subdued the assassin. The next day at the local hospital, after he said his last words to his wife: "I do not want them to undress me . . . I want you to undress me," she calmed him with what were to be their last kisses, and Leon Trotsky died that evening. He was sixty-one years old.

BATTLE OF BRITAIN

Last Day: Hitler's incessant air attacks directed at English cities, called the Battle of Britain, ended on October 31, 1940.

Background: The Battle of Britain began in May 1940, heated up by July, and intensified through August, with the fiercest fighting occurring between August 30 and September 7. In that crucial period the skies over Britain had become thunderous as raging dogfights ensued between Hitler's Messerschmitts and British Spitfires and

Hawker Hurricanes. Passing beyond the thin RAF ranks, German planes bombed channel shipping and pounded British coastal regions before moving inland, causing death and destruction as they bombarded cities to ruin and rubble.

The turning point of the Battle of Britain came when RAF planes on September 15 shot down fifty-six Messerschmitts as the Germans began their notorious London Blitz. By October Germany's losses were staggering, with more than two thousand planes downed, while the RAF had lost eight hundred planes. By mid-October the German losses climbed to twenty-three hundred planes. Germany's main problem in the Battle of Britain was that her planes had to cut off their attacks, often in the thick of an engagement, to return to French bases while they still had enough fuel. As fewer and fewer German planes crossed over from France, the British realized that the Battle of Britain was winding down. By the end of October the Luftwaffe had failed to show up for some ten days. On October 31, 1940, the Battle of Britain was over. Germany had had her first taste of defeat. Pilots of Canada, the United States, Norway, and Israel had participated in the Battle of Britain against the Germans. Of the battle, British Prime Minister Winston Churchill said: "Never in the field of human conflict was so much owed by so many to so few."

PETER II

Last Monarch of Yugoslavia: King Peter II was forced to flee his kingdom on April 6, 1941, during the Nazi occupation, when his troops were defeated by German forces. The monarchy was abolished in 1945, and a republic was proclaimed with Marshall Josef Tito as prime minister.

Background: Peter came to the United States after the war, where he lived in exile and wrote *A King's Heritage* in 1954. He hoped to return to Yugoslavia. Peter II died at age forty-seven in 1970.

TOWER OF LONDON

Last Execution: The captured spy Josef Jakobs was shot by a firing squad at the Tower of London on August 14, 1941.

SIMEON II

Last Monarch of Bulgaria: Simeon II, young son of Czar Boris III, in 1943 succeeded his father, who died under mysterious circumstances.

Background: Czar Simeon II, a nominal ruler under a regency, never reigned, due to the Russian invasion in 1943 and an eventual plebiscite that paved the way for a Soviet-type People's Republic and the abolition of the monarchy. Born in 1937, Simeon II lives in Madrid, Spain.

LADY BE GOOD

Last Diary Entries by Lieutenant R. F. Toner: "Sunday April 4 Naples—28 planes—things well mixed up—got lost returning, out of gas, jumped, landed in desert at 2 a.m. morning, no one hurt, can't find John, all others resem [reassembled].

Monday April 5, start walking now, still no John, a few rations ½ canteen of water, one cup full per day. Sun fairly warm. Good breeze from NW. Nite very cold. No sleep, rested and walked [a canteen cup holds little more than a thimbleful of water].

Tues. April 6, rested at 11:30, sun very warm no breeze, spent PM in hell, no planes etc. Rested until 5 P.M. very warm, hell. Everyone can't sleep, walked and rested all nite. 15 min on, 5 min. off.

Wed. April 7, same routine, everyone getting weak, can't get very far, prayers all the time, again P.M. very warm, hell. Everyone can't sleep, everyone sore from gout.

Mon. April 12: No hope yet, very cold night."

Background: A couple of British geologists were trekking over sand dunes in the Libyan desert in early May 1959 when they came upon a strange find. In a region known as the Sand Sea of Calanscio, they discovered a derelict giant World War II B-24 United States Liberator Bomber. A look inside the plane revealed full water jugs, unused ammunition, rations, fatigue clothes, flight gear, and a radio in perfect condition. All that was missing were the plane's occupants.

The geologist did not know it at the time, but what they had discovered would eventually answer one of the most baffling mysteries of World War II, according to the U.S. Air Force: the disappearance of a bomber with Tail Number 124301, better known as the *Lady Be Good*. Word went out from Libya to the U.S. Air Force headquarters at Wiesbaden, West Germany. United States investigative teams in Europe and Africa were dispatched to the scene and World War II Pentagon records were dusted off and studied. By the end of June the air force had begun to piece together the mystery: The plane was indeed the missing and unaccounted for *Lady Be Good*.

The *Lady Be Good*—so named by its crew of nine—had taken off from an isolated airstrip in the Libyan desert twenty-eight miles from Benghazi on April 4, 1943; its destination, Naples, Italy, for a bombing mission. The plane and its crew were never seen or heard from again. One year later the next of kin were notified that their sons and husbands were missing in action. The *Lady Be Good*'s log book did not indicate the crew members or note whether it had completed its mission or what course it was on. The air force had the names of the crew and theorized that they had parachuted from the plane when the bomber's fuel became dangerously low and had perished in the desert. The belly landing on the soft sand had not damaged the plane. The air force proved to be correct—but they would also learn of a tale of despair and hardship, for a diary was found revealing the terrible fate of the nine crew members: pilot Lieutenant William J. Hatton of Queens, New York; Lieutenant Robert F. Toner of Massachusetts; Lieutenant D. P. Hayes of Missouri; Lieutenant John S. Woravka of Ohio; Sergeant Harold S. Ripslinger of Michigan; Sergeant Robert E. Lamotte of Michigan; Sergeant Guy E. Shelley of Pennsylvania; Sergeant Vernon L. Moore of Ohio;

and Sergeant Samuel R. Adams of Illinois. A search for the remains of the missing airmen was immediately undertaken, with reconnaissance planes making maps of the region.

For seven months no trace of the fliers was uncovered, and then in February 1960, due to shifting sand dunes, five of the missing fliers were found. On the skeletal remains of Lieutenant Robert F. Toner was found a little black diary in which he had penciled in the events that brought the plane and crew to its fate. Toner revealed that after they parachuted into the desert at night, Lieutenant John Woravka was not with them. They never saw him again.

All but one of the nine deceased airmen were eventually recovered from the desert. The body of Vernon L. Moore was never found.

LESLIE HOWARD

Last Seen: Leslie Howard was last seen boarding a British transport plane at Lisbon Airport in Portugal on June 1, 1943.

Background: The British actor Leslie Howard, remembered for his roles as Ashley Wilkes in *Gone With the Wind,* and as the Scarlet Pimpernel in the French Revolution film, had the misfortune of having an accountant who looked like Winston Churchill. Asked by the British War Council to be a goodwill ambassador, the handsome, soft-spoken actor decided to take his cigar-smoking accountant and close friend Alfred Chenhalls with him. Together with twelve other civilian passengers, Howard and Chenhalls boarded a British Overseas Airway transport plane for a flight from Lisbon to London. The date was June 1, 1943. Near noon, over the Atlantic in the Gulf of Gascony near the coast of France, the pilot of the flight became concerned when he saw eight German fighter planes droning not far behind. Less than a half hour later the pilot desperately sent the message: "We are being attacked." Communications broke off. Search planes combed the entire area, but no trace of the British transport was ever seen. Winston Churchill had always been a target of assassination, and officials believe that the attack was a case of mistaken identity by German agents who thought they had spotted Churchill boarding the British transport at Lisbon.

BATTLE OF MONTE CASSINO

Last Day: The battle of Monte Cassino ended on May 18, 1944.

Background: The battle for the road to Rome, between crack German paratroopers and American, English, New Zealand, Polish, and Indian soldiers, began in mid-January 1944. At center stage was a Roman Catholic abbey perched high up on a mountain overlooking the Lire Valley held by the Germans. For some three months hundreds of Allied soldiers lost their lives in an attempt to dislodge the enemy. The surrounding town of Monte Cassino itself had been a terrible battleground with a high loss of life on both sides. Suddenly the Allies were stopped—unable to proceed and link up with Allied forces at Anzio. No amount of firepower could dislodge the Germans from their mountain fortification, while the casualties kept piling up.

With the road to Rome blocked, on February 9, 1944, word came from the U.S. High Command that the only alternative left to the Allies was to bomb the monastery. The monastery was bombed on February 17, and from the outside world, not familiar with the facts, outrage was immediate. The first bombings did not dislodge the Germans, nor did future assaults in which tons of bombs and plane strafings rocked the mountain. The German paratroopers only used the rubble and bomb craters as protection in their defense. From partially intact walls, massive stone pillars, and heaps of brick, they fired tens of thousands of rounds from automatic rifles and submachine guns and lobbed stick grenades down the mountainside, killing surging troops by the hundreds. The mountainside was laden with dead and wounded, and no amount of air strafing could break the enemy stronghold.

Meanwhile the few monks who insisted on staying in the monastery, risking their lives, took sanctuary in the deep cellars of the abbey, though most had agreed to leave weeks before the siege on the advice of the German commander, himself a Catholic, who had expected the devastating offensive. Through May the last of the bombs were dropped, but it was up to ground troops to break the stalemate as air strikes were proving useless. The mountain abbey was holding up the Allied advance, and though the German command did not know it, the road to Rome was being watched across the world in Washington. Roosevelt knew why the mountain fortification had to fall and why soldiers would have to keep dying until the Germans were dislodged.

Hitler suspected a second front might open up in Italy, and holding the mountain was vital to his plan to close the important road to Rome. Pope Pius XII, who had received the abbot of Monte Cassino, Bishop Gregorio Diamare, the night of the initial bombing, comforted the abbott when he was told by General Mark Clark that bombing the monastery was a military necessity.

On the night of May 17 the mountain was quiet. Firepower from the broken monastery was nil. On the morning of May 18 Polish soldiers scaled the mount unhindered. The devastation they beheld was unbelievable. Amid bomb craters, some dead soldiers, smoldering rubble, cases of ammunition, and tens of thousands of shells were a few tired soldiers. Most of the paratroopers had escaped overnight. Monte Cassino was there for the taking; the road to Rome was open.

After the war the Benedictine Abbey of Monte Cassino was rebuilt. On October 24, 1964, Pope Paul VI consecrated the new monastery.

ANNE FRANK
Last Paragraph of Diary Entry (August 1, 1944): "A voice sobs within me: 'There you are, that's what's become of you: you're uncharitable, you look supercilious and peevish, people dislike you and all because you won't listen

to the advice given you by your own better half.' Oh, I would like to listen, but it doesn't work; if I'm quiet and serious, everyone thinks it's a new comedy and then I have to get out of it by turning it into a joke, not to mention my own family, who are sure to think I'm ill, make me swallow pills for headaches and nerves, feel my neck and my head to see whether I'm running a temperature, ask if I'm constipated and criticize me for being in a bad mood. I can't keep that up: if I'm watched to that extent, I start by getting snappy, then unhappy, and finally I twist my heart round again, so that the bad is on the outside and the good is on the inside and keep on trying to find a way of becoming what I would so like to be, and what I could be, if . . . there weren't any other people living in the world.

Yours, Anne.''

Background: Anne Frank was born on June 12, 1929, in Frankfurt, Germany. Her childhood and early adolescence were happy, with loving parents, close school friends, and the marvelous beginning of sexual awakening. But upheaval was on the way. The little girl who had so much to live for, who dreamed, laughed, and sorrowed as all youngsters do, was Jewish. This fact alone would cost her her life before her sixteenth birthday. Seeing the storm clouds darkening Germany, Anne's father Otto Frank, took his wife, Anne, and her sister Margot out of his homeland, fleeing to Amsterdam, Holland.

In 1940, with the world spinning toward a global war, Holland was one of the first casualties as the Nazis invaded the Netherlands. In 1942 Otto Frank took his family to the upstairs back of his former food emporium, where an annex had already been prepared for living conditions. Mr. and Mrs. Frank, Anne, and Margot were joined by four other Jews who feared for their lives. They were Mr. and Mrs. Van Daan and their son Peter, and a dentist named Albert Dussel. With friends on the outside, the eight occupants managed to survive. The quarters were cramped, and during the day, with a business being conducted in the lower part of the building, where the public was in and out, the occupants had to follow strict rules of silence while confining their movements to a minimum.

History might never have known of this situation were it not for Anne, who was only thirteen years old, but extremely bright. Somewhat reluctant to share her feeling with others, she began to keep a diary on June 14, 1942. The diary consisted of letters to Kitty, a name Anne invented because it sounded friendly. The famous diary contains almost two hundred letters, full of observations about the war, Hitler, the Allies, classical composers, growing up, her surroundings, the other occupants—she noted that Dussel "is beginning to get lonely for women," and that some of the occupants ate too much. A radio kept all abreast of events in the outside world, and one entry expresses joy that it was a German who attempted to assassinate Hitler with a bomb. She commented on her friends of school days, the bickering among some of the occupants, and the gap between the grownups and her sister, herself, and Peter.

And then Anne began a new and exciting experience: She and Peter discovered each other. They fell in love. In Anne Frank's last entry of her diary, Tuesday, August 1, 1944, she referred to herself as a "bundle of contradictions." Anne proceeded to admonish herself for showing people her bad side, lest they think her better than they. The last entry betrayed no hint of foreboding as she thought the Allies were winning victories against Germany. The broadcasts were optimistic and Anne and the other seven occupants were alive and hoped that they would soon emerge from their confinement as free people.

On August 4, 1944, the Gestapo penetrated the secret annex after an informant gave the police the location of the hiding place. All the eight occupants were arrested and sent to Auschwitz in Poland. In Auschwitz the men and women were separated. After three months, Anne, Margot, and Mrs. Van Daan were selected to be transferred to Belsen concentration camp in Germany. Mrs. Frank, left behind in Auschwitz, lost her will to live. Refusing to eat, she became so weak that her guards placed her in the camp infirmary, where she died. Mr. Van Daan was gassed to death. Mr. Dussel died under the extreme privation at Neurengamme camp in Germany. Young Peter Van Daan was taken from Auschwitz by the Germans when they fled the camp after the invasion by Russian soldiers. He was never seen or heard from again.

At Belsen camp, Anne's school friend, Lies Goosens, met Anne early in 1945, only days before Anne died. Goosens' account: "I waited shivering in the darkness. It took a long time, but suddenly I heard a voice: 'Lies, Lies, where are you?' It was Anne, and I ran in the direction of the voice, and then I saw her beyond the barbed wire. She was in rags. I saw her emaciated, sunken face in darkness. Her eyes were large. We cried and cried, for now there was only barbed wire between us, nothing more, and no longer any difference in our fates. I told Anne that my mother had died and my father was dying, and Anne told me that she knew nothing about her father, but her mother had been left behind in Auschwitz. Only Margot was still with her but she was already very sick. They had not seen Mrs. Van Daan again after her arrival at Belsen."

Anne's sister, Margot, and Mrs. Van Daan died before Anne, though she did not know of their deaths. Anne did suspect that her sister was gone. She did not know that her mother had died. Soon after their deaths, in early March 1945, before her sixteenth birthday, Anne Frank died peacefully. Otto Frank, the lone surviver of the secret annex, returned to Amsterdam, Holland, after the war. There, friends gave him his family possessions. With the returned items was his daughter Anne's diary.

GLENN MILLER

Last Seen: Orchestra leader Glen Miller boarded a C-64 Norseman light plane from London to Paris on December 15, 1944.

Background: Major Glenn Miller, who had joined the Army on October 7, 1942 to entertain the troops with his band, had other things on his mind besides music on December 15, 1944. He had just boarded a C-64 nine-seat Norseman light plane at London, bound for Paris to entertain French and English troops, when he began inquiring about the absence of parachutes—not standard equipment on such planes, which usually performed short flights. A colonel friend ribbed the trombonist with: "What's the matter, Miller? Do you want to live forever?" With strict radio silence prevailing because of the impending Battle of the Bulge, in damp, drizzling conditions, the single-engine plane took off from an airfield near Bedford, London. Glenn Miller, age forty, and three other persons were never seen again. On December 24, 1944, the famous bandleader and the other passengers were officially declared lost at sea.

BATTLE OF THE BULGE

Last Day: On December 27, 1944, General Patton's Third Army stopped the Nazi advance after relieving General McAuliffe's troops following the siege of Bastogne.

Background: The Battle of the Bulge—Germans versus the Allies in Belgium-Luxembourg territory—was so named after a "bulge" sixty miles deep was created by a fierce German drive. In the wooded plateau region known as the Ardennes Forest, an American airborne division occupying the strategic town of Bastogne, vital because of its railroad and highway junction, was surrounded as a result of a surprise German offensive under the command of Marshal von Rundstedt, who launched his drive on December 16, 1944. The Germans inflicted very high casualties in their lightning offensive. Fog made Allied air strikes impossible and created an enormous salient in the Allied lines that came to be called a bulge. The Ardennes offensive would have ended in success for the Germans were it not for the lifting of the fog.

Indeed, on December 21 Rundstedt sent General Anthony McAuliffe an ultimatum of surrender. McAuliffe's reply became historic, not only for its brevity, but also for its audacity. The reply was one word: "Nuts!" The famous reply would have seemed foolish but for the lifting of the fog, which permitted air strikes that saturated German positions, the strikes taking place on December 24. With Rundstedt unable to supply his forces and with the advance and arrival of Patton's units on December 27, 1944, the Battle of the Bulge was over. The Ardennes offensive was officially ended on January 16, 1945, after British and American forces caused a German abandonment of their Ardennes venture on January 8. The Ardennes German counteroffensive was Hitler's last offensive. A staggering 77,000 Allied soldiers lost their lives in the Ardennes campaign.

EDDIE SLOVIK

Last American Soldier Executed for Desertion: Private Eddie Slovik, age twenty-five, was executed on January 31, 1945.

Background: Finding the men to make up the firing squad proved difficult, since no one would volunteer. The squad forced to perform the detail was told that only one rifle would be loaded and the others would contain blanks. The soldier firing the loaded rifle was not supposed to know he had executed Slovik.

FRANKLIN DELANO ROOSEVELT

(Thirty-second President of the United States)

Last Day of Life: Franklin Roosevelt died on April 12, 1945, early in his fourth term as president.

Background: FDR, as Roosevelt was known, had contracted poliomyelitis in 1921, and until his death he was confined to a wheelchair. By the time he was in his third term the Depression that had greeted him in his first term as president was fading from the American scene as his various New Deal programs had restored a healthier economic climate. But FDR knew great turmoil in his last years as president: Pearl Harbor was attacked on December 7, 1941, the Manhattan Project resulted in the construction of an atomic bomb, and thousands of American soldiers died in Europe and the Pacific. The Normandy invasion and names like Hitler, Mussolini, Japan's Hideki Tojo and Hirohito were to occupy his mind day and night.

FDR began to suffer from high blood pressure and poor appetite. The last day of the president's life started off well enough. He was preparing to have his portrait painted that morning at his Warm Springs cottage in Georgia, on April 12, 1945. As he exchanged parlor-talk pleasantries with his two women guests while lunch was being served, at 12:45 P.M., FDR's face took on an expression of fatigue and became noticeably pale. Lifting his head as if to stretch, he fell back in his chair. The screams of his guests brought some of the household staff and his doctor to his side. Roosevelt said his last words in the presence of his house boy: "I have a terrific headache." As Roosevelt lost consciousness, the doctor took his blood pressure and administered a solution of amyl nitrite, but the thirty-second president never regained consciousness. FDR was pronounced dead at 3:30 in the afternoon, having suffered a cerebral hemorrhage. Born in Hyde Park, New York, on January 30, 1882, he was sixty-three years old.

Franklin and Eleanor Roosevelt had five sons and one daughter. FDR loved to go sailing, and his favorite place on earth was his estate of Hyde Park, New York. He had a way with words: "Happy days are here again." "I see one-third of a nation ill-housed, ill-clad, ill-nourished." "The only thing we have to fear is fear itself." "We look forward to a world founded upon four essential human freedoms . . . freedom of speech and expression . . . freedom of every person to worship God in his own way . . .freedom from want . . . freedom from fear . . ." FDR is a symbol of the greatness in the American presidency.

Gravesite: The Roosevelt Home, Hyde Park, New York.

BENITO MUSSOLINI

Last Day of Life: The Italian Fascist premier was executed on April 28, 1945.

Background: On September 8, 1943, with Italy having surrendered to the Allies, Mussolini was finished as a dictator. However, with the aid of Hitler, the Axis continued to occupy and fight in Italy, with two great battles yet to be fought—Anzio and Monte Cassino.

Mussolini languished for almost two years in a mountain prison before he was freed by German troops and proceeded to run a puppet government. With the eventual fall of Germany, Mussolini had nowhere to go. The American and English armies were surging to his doorstep when Mussolini managed to escape to Milan, Italy. Attempts to escape his country into Germany failed, and Mussolini and his mistress Claretta Petacci were prisoners. Within hours after his capture on April 28, 1945, an Italian military court sentenced Mussolini, his mistress, and a dozen members of his entouage to death by firing squad. That afternoon, only hours after sentence was pronounced, the military court's mandate was carried out. Benito Mussolini was executed at 4 o'clock. Some scholars remember Benito Mussolini for nothing more than making the trains of Italy run on time.

Born in 1883, the Italian dictator and leader of Italy's Fascist movement was called Il Duce, meaning "the leader." Mussolini came to power after 1922 when King Victor Emmanuel called on him to form a cabinet. He had made the mistake of attacking Ethiopia in 1935, an act that isolated Italy from the world community. Mussolini at first had opposed Germany's Adolf Hitler but, ostracized by the world, the Italian dictator was forced to accept a political alliance with Germany, becoming part of the Axis powers against the Allies. But Mussolini was a poor leader. As head of the Fascist party (Fascist from the old Roman word *Fasces,* which meant a bundle of rods and axes for disciplining lawbreakers), he promoted suppression and militarism, like the Nazis of Germany.

ADOLF HITLER

Last Day of Life: German chancellor and Fuhrer Adolf Hitler died on April 30, 1945.

Background: Adolf Hitler's final months of life were lived in extreme mental and physical pain. An attempt made on the Fuhrer's life on July 20, 1944, when a bomb explosion failed to kill him, did inflict minor injuries, among these a shattered eardrum that caused him much prolonged pain. Hitler was well aware that his nation was losing the war, a realization that caused his health to deteriorate. He was in agony over such defeats as El Alamein in the Egyptian desert (October 24–November 4, 1942), which cost him Africa. There were the staggering defeats in Russia, the Normandy invasion, and his last hope, the Ardennes offensive that became the Battle of the Bulge and ended in German defeat on December 27, 1944. It had finally dawned on Hitler that he was not invincible, and that some of his most trusted confidants were not loyal enough to die with him in his last sanctuary, a bunker under the battle-ravaged city of Berlin.

Only days before he took his life, the Fuhrer's sweetheart, Eva Braun, had come to his hideaway to be with him—against Hitler's wishes. Hitler was deeply touched. Braun could have gained safe passage out of war-torn Germany to South America—an option exercised by some top Third Reich leaders—but instead chose to die with her beloved.

On April 29, 1945, Hitler and Eva Braun were married. After the wedding the Fuhrer and his bride retired to a private sitting room of the bunker to plan a suicide pact. After drawing up a will, they set the time for taking their lives for April 30, 1945, at 3:30 in the afternoon. Time was short. The Russian army was moving on Berlin from the east of Germany, the Allies from the west. Tank fire, machine gun fire, and bombs were exploding above the bunker, located under the almost destroyed chancellery. One by one, German strongholds fell under flames, while artillery fire caused Berlin's buildings to crumble. Snipers, civilians, and soldiers ran for their lives as the Russians converged on Berlin.

In the damp bunker, heavy with the odor of cement and the muffled poundings of the carnage of the battle in the city, Hitler and Braun looked toward the time of 3:30. Those outside his sitting room heard a loud gunshot from a Walther pistol. Within moments the Fuhrer's valet entered the death room. What he saw was momentarily horrifying: Hitler and Braun were in a sitting position on a sofa. Blood poured from a ghastly hole in Hitler's right temple where the powerful Walther bullet had penetrated. It was not clear if Hitler's wound had been self-inflicted or if Braun had shot the Fuhrer. Two Walther pistols were found at the death scene. It was also discovered that Hitler had bit on a cyanide capsule and may have suffered convulsions. Eva Braun had died from cyanide.

Hitler's aides quickly collected the bodies, hastened to a courtyard, and drenched the corpses in petrol before setting them on fire. With the city under siege, the bodies were allowed to burn to a charred state and were dragged to a shallow burial site near the chancellery.

The Russians under the command of Marshal Georgi Zhukov were first on the scene. After they unearthed Hitler's and Braun's remains, the Russians issued a statement to the Allies that both were dead. Then, for reasons known only to Zhukov and the Russian high command, the Russians retracted their statement, claiming instead that they had not found Hitler and Braun. The Russian fabrication thus gave rise to the legend that Hitler had survived and escaped to South America.

No man in the history of mankind, save for Jesus Christ, is more widely written of than Adolf Hitler. Hitler was born to an unwed woman named Anna Maria Schicklgruber on April 20, 1889, in Braunau in Upper Austria. The name on his birth certificate is Adolfus Hitler, son of Alois Hitler—hence, his actual last name was Hitler and not Schicklgruber as is often believed. He had an uneventful childhood in which he was raised a Roman Catholic—and even thought of becoming a priest after he failed to gain admittance into Austria's Academy of Fine Arts, Vienna, for the study of architectural art.

With World War I upon Germany, Hitler enlisted in the Bavarian army. Winner of the German Iron Cross, he emerged from the war a bitter man, blaming Germany's defeat on the Jews and the Marxists. Shortly after the war, Hitler became chairman of the new National Socialist Workers' Party, or Nazi Party, in 1919. Using violence, the Nazis systematically eliminated opposition to its goals—mainly racism against Jews. The principal aim of the party was to rearm Germany and bring the fallen nation back to being the most powerful country on the face of the earth.

Hitler's quest for world power was temporarily interrupted when he drew a prison sentence for his part in the attempt to overthrow the Bavarian government in what became known as the Munich Putsch or Beer Hall Putsch (*putsch* means "insurrection"). While Hitler was in prison he outlined his philosophy in a 1923 book entitled *Mein Kampf* (*My Struggle*). Leaving prison after serving nine months of a five-year sentence, Hitler was considered a hero by many. *Mein Kampf* became a bestseller and required reading by all loyal Germans during Hitler's rise to chancellor of Germany.

When Chancellor Kurt von Schleicher resigned his post in the face of civil upheaval in Germany, President Paul von Hindenburg made Hitler chancellor on January 30, 1933. Seeking to become the dictator of Germany, Hitler faced opposition from the Communist Party. A terrible fire on February 27, 1933, clearly started by Hitler's henchmen, resulted in the German Parliament building, or Reichstag, burning to the ground. Hitler blamed the fire on the Communists, turning public opinion against them. In subsequent elections on March 5, 1933, the Nazi regime took the majority of seats, and Adolf Hitler's power as dictator of Germany was nearly complete. After the death of von Hindenburg on August 2, 1934, a plebiscite in which Hitler gained 88 percent of the German vote gave him supreme power over the fate of Germany; he was the Fuhrer of the German people. His regime was to be known as the Third Reich (Third Empire), which Hitler said would last a thousand years. Upon his final triumph to absolute power in Germany, Hitler began his scheme to bring Germany to world dominance. Through propaganda minister Josef Goebbels and cabinet ministers Hermann Goering and Heinrich Himmler (head of the dreaded Gestapo), Hitler was ready to undertake his goals. On March 7, 1936, German forces reoccupied the Rhineland; Austria was next to fall to Hitler when he annexed the country of his birth in March 1936. Shortly after, the Sudetenland and Czechoslovakia were signed over to Hitler, allowing him to occupy these territories, on September 30, 1938, as a gesture of appeasement, according to English Prime Minister Neville Chamberlain. In Germany, in a vicious quest to establish a "master (Aryan) race," a Nazi campaign was under way that would result in the establishment of death camps where millions of Jews and other supposed undesirables would eventually be exterminated. The invasion of Poland was next on Hitler's timetable of conquest. Hitler's invasion of Poland on September 1, 1939, was the opening salvo that sparked the outbreak of World War II.

KARL DOENITZ

Last Fuhrer: Karl Doenitz succeeded Adolf Hitler after his death on April 30, 1945, to become the last Fuhrer of Nazi Germany. He held the office for twenty-three days.

Background: The chief naval commander before becoming Fuhrer, Doenitz spearheaded the drive to make German sea power a mighty force from 1935 through 1943. Under his command, the dreaded wolfpacks—an assembly of U-boats, as many as seventy-five to a pack— were responsible for destroying Allied shipping, sinking convoys and their escorts into the millions of tons. Doenitz negotiated Germany's surrender and was later sentenced to nine years in Spandau for war crimes. No fervent Nazi like Erwin Rommel, Doenitz was a soldier endowed with a most brilliant military mind and a splendid sea tactician who gave Germany a submarine force second to none. Upon his release from Spandau, he lived quietly in Aumuhle, West Germany, until his death of a heart attack on December 24, 1980, at age eighty-nine.

WORLD WAR II

Last Day: On September 2, 1945, on the battleship *Missouri* in Tokyo, Japan, Japanese delegates signed a formal document of surrender. In Europe, World War II ended on May 8, 1945, one day after the German high command surrendered unconditionally to the Allies; the surrender was signed near Rheims, France.

Background: Adolf Hitler, head of the Third Reich, a World War I veteran, began his scheme to abrogate the Treaty of Versailles, which had left Germany on the brink of economic disaster after World War I. In 1935 Hitler began his quest to restore Germany to greatness by announcing the installation of a compulsory draft of young German boys—a violation of the armament clauses of the Versailles Treaty. In 1936 Hitler made his boldest move by marching troops into the Rhineland. By the end of 1936 Germany had allied herself with Italy in a Rome-Berlin Axis.

On September 1, 1939, Germany invaded Poland, and by so doing precipitated the most costly war in history. Two days later, Great Britain and France declared war on Germany. Holland and little Belgium fell to the mighty German Panzer (tank) divisions, and on June 14, 1940, France fell. It was from France that Germany launched her air attacks against Great Britain in what became known as the Battle of Britain. In 1941 the German army moved upon the Balkans. Hungary, Bulgaria, and Romania joined Hitler, increasing the might of the Axis. In that same year Germany broke across Russian frontiers. Japan and the United States came into the war on December 7, 1941, when Japan bombed the U.S. Pacific fleet at Pearl Harbor, bringing an immediate declaration of war from the United States, who with Great Britain, France, and Russia became the Allies.

Germany was weakened because of the United States entry into World War II. The tide turned against her in 1943 with her stunning defeat in North Africa when Field Marshal Rommel surrendered with his army of three hundred thousand soldiers after running out of food and fuel for their massive tank corps. Germany's push deep inside Russia during the bitter winter of 1943 cost her half a million men, while Italy under Benito Mussolini fell apart after the U.S. and British paratroop drop in Sicily. On June 6, 1944, Operation Overlord, the great armada of ships and planes, besieged the beaches of Normandy, France, in what became known as D Day, an undertaking skillfully supervised by General Dwight D. Eisenhower, the supreme Allied commander.

Hitler's last offensive was mounted in December 1944 in what became known as the Battle of the Bulge. It failed. With Russian troops closing in on Berlin, with Benito Mussolini having been executed on April 28, 1945, the Third Reich was finished. In a bunker under the Reich chancellery, Adolf Hitler took his life. Europe was left in ruins. With the discovery of internment camps where the Nazis gassed millions of Jews, the madness of the Third Reich was realized.

The war in Asia still blazed, with thousands dying, with Iwo Jima and Okinawa becoming the final battlegrounds. In the end, after the United States dropped two atomic bombs—one on the city of Hiroshima on August 6, 1945, and another on the city of Nagasaki on August 9, 1945, each claiming an immediate one hundred thousand lives, Japan surrendered. World War II had taken fifty-four million lives, mostly civilians.

ZOGU I

Last Monarch of Albania: King Zogu I, having proclaimed himself king in 1938, fled in 1939 when Benito Mussolini's forces invaded his nation. He abdicated in 1943, and his monarchy was officially abolished in 1946 when, under a Communist regime, Albania was proclaimed a People's Republic.

Background: Ahmed Bey Zogu (also known as Scanderbeg III) was born in 1895. He was a Sunni Muslim who held important state posts before his proclamation as king, including president of Albania. Known simply as Zog, he died in France in 1961 at age sixty-six. Zog smoked twelve packs of cigarettes a day.

HUMBERT II

Last Monarch of Italy: King Humbert II, the former prince of Piedmont, abdicated and went into exile on June 13, 1946, when a plebiscite paved the way for a republic.

Background: King Humbert II was the son of Victor Emmanuel III. Born in 1904, he lived in Portugal as Count Sarre. Humbert II died in 1983.

WILLIE SUTTON

Last Prison Escape: Bank robber Willie Sutton escaped from the maximum-security Holmsburg County Jail in Philadelphia, Pennsylvania, on February 9, 1947. In a fierce snowstorm, Sutton managed to reach New York City.

Background: Born in 1901 in Brooklyn, New York, Sutton is famous for a remark he claimed never to have made: "I rob banks because that's where the money is." Sutton's career spanned over twenty-five years. When he was committing his crimes—mostly robbing banks—Sutton liked to remind his victims that they would recover their losses by telling them, "Don't worry, the insurance will cover this." He never took a life. Sutton is remembered for his disguises, hence the nickname Willie the Actor. In addition to robbing banks, he also was a jewel thief and safecracker. He was nabbed for the last time in 1952 after being spotted on a New York City subway by a salesman named Arnold Schuster, who followed him to a gas station and called the police. FBI agents arrested Sutton. On March 7, 1952, an unknown gunman shot Schuster to death near his Brooklyn home. Schuster's family won a damage suit from New York City in the 1970s. Sutton is the subject of two biographies: *I Willie Sutton* by Quentin Reynolds (1955) and *Where the Money Was,* by Edward Linn (1976).

AL CAPONE

Last Day of Life: Having been struck with apoplexy, Al Capone was surrounded by his family when he died suddenly of heart failure in Miami, Florida, on February 25, 1947. He was forty-eight years old.

BUGSY SIEGEL

Last Day of Life: Bugsy Siegel was murdered on July 20, 1947.

Background: On orders from mob king Lucky Luciano, unhappy over Siegel's unpaid debts, Bugsy Siegel was killed on July 20, 1947, in Los Angeles, California. As he sat amid the sumptuous opulence of a Beverly Hills mansion owned by his girlfriend, Virginia Hill, a sniper with a powerful 30-30 rifle sent three shots through a window, the bullets blowing away half of Siegel's handsome face and killing him instantly.

MICHAEL I

Last Monarch of Romania: King Michael I abdicated on December 30, 1947, when a Communist bloc government was voted into power.

Background: In 1948 Michael I married Princess Anne of Bourbon-Parma. Today Michael I, a businessman, has not entirely given up the dream of once again returning to his beloved homeland.

MOHANDAS GANDHI

Last Day of Life: Gandhi was assassinated on January 30, 1948.

Background: Called Mahatma by his followers—a title that means "great soul," Gandhi preached nonviolence and through prayer and fasting was responsible for gaining Indian independence. However, the India-Pakistan partition brought about by the Hindu leader did not please certain Indian political factions, and one man, a disgruntled newspaper editor named Nathuram Vinayak, stole a piece of India's history.

On the evening of January 30, 1948, the frail leader who preached passive resistance, flanked by his grandnieces, was moving through his Birla House Gardens in New Delhi, India. On his way to a prayer meeting, Gandhi, weak from fasting, needed assistance with each stride. As the aged leader moved through the grounds, a great mass of admirers paid him homage with much weeping, wailing, and surging to touch his white garments.

Almost overwhelmed by the emotional throng, Gandhi was suddenly unable to move when a young man blocked his path. As the revered figure waited to receive a gesture of respect, the man, Nathuram Vinayak, shoved Gandhi off stride, causing his two female escorts to lose their grasp on his arms. Vinayak produced a gun, and fired point-blank. The first of four shots struck Gandhi in the lower stomach; two more bullets hit him in the chest. Dropping to his knees, the wounded Gandhi clutched his stomach. The enraged mob set upon the assailant, and only Gandhi's pleading motions spared Vinayak for the authorities. Within twenty minutes after being shot, Mohandas Karamchand Gandhi, his lips moving in prayer, died. Born in 1863 at Forbander, India, Gandhi was seventy-eight years old.

BABE RUTH

Last Day of Life: Babe Ruth died on August 16, 1948.

Background: Suffering from throat cancer for more than a year, Ruth was admitted into the Memorial Hospital in New York City. He received more than fifty thousand letters and cards from well-wishers, including a personal note from President Truman. Many great sports figures and dignitaries came to see him. On the night of August

16, 1948, with mobs of children keeping vigil outside the hospital, Ruth was whispering some prayers when he sank into a coma. His family at his bedside watched and waited in prayer as Babe received the last rites of the Roman Catholic Church. Then at 8 P.M. the immortal baseball star was pronounced dead. He was fifty-three years old.

AQUITANIA

Last Voyage: The *Aquitania*'s last voyage ended on December 1, 1949.

Background: Few luxury liners received the advance publicity of the *Aquitania,* and bookings were quickly filled for her maiden voyage in 1914. She had a long and eventful life, and was the last of the four-funnel vessels. She had classic picture-book looks and might easily have been mistaken for the *Titanic.* With six decks, she could accommodate three thousand people. Converted to battle status in World War I, the *Aquitania* was used to transport troops to the Dardanelles. Afterward she was returned to luxury trans-Atlantic service, but was again used by the British in World War II. She gave much pleasure to her passengers after World War II, but began showing signs of aging, and died at the scrapyard at Garelock, Scotland, on December 19, 1949.

WILLIE SUTTON

Last Bank Robbery: With two cohorts, Willie Sutton held up the Manufacturers Trust Company Bank in Sunnyside, Queens, New York City, on March 9, 1950, escaping with $63,933. No one was hurt.

GEORGE WASHINGTON

Last Year: In 1951, the ship was doomed to the scrap heap.

Background: Launched in 1909 and originally owned by Germany under the same name, she was nicknamed Big George. Seized by the United States prior to World War

I, she was pressed into service as a troop ship. After the war the *George Washington* carried President Wilson to the Versailles Peace Conference. In World War II the *George Washington* was again pressed into military service under the British colors; perhaps remembering the American Revolution, the British changed her name to the *Catlin*. The United States got her back in 1943, restoring the name *George Washington*. She had a fairly good speed of nineteen knots and was able to accommodate twenty-five hundred passengers. On January 16, 1951, a fire doomed her.

FAROUK

Last Monarch of Egypt: King Farouk abdicated on July 26, 1952, after a sixteen-year reign, giving way to an eventual republic on June 18, 1953. King Farouk was called the last pharoah. His abdication came in the face of a coup d'etat led by General Muhammad Naguib.

Background: King Farouk left his kingdom in such a hurry that among his abandoned personal effects was found a rare American coin—a $20 gold piece that had mysteriously vanished from a Philadelphia museum. A compulsive gambler who used chips that were never worth less than $2,000, he often lost $200,000 during his sprees at Monaco's gambling establishments. The palace of the last king of Egypt is now a museum. Born in 1920, King Farouk succeeded his father, Ahmed Fuad I, who died in 1936. Farouk died in 1965 at age forty-five.

HARRY S TRUMAN
(Thirty-third President of the United States)

Last Day in Office: January 20, 1953, after almost two terms. Truman became the thirty-third president upon the death of Franklin D. Roosevelt.

Background: Vice President Truman was summoned to the White House on April 12, 1945, and ushered into Eleanor Roosevelt's study. The First Lady smiled bravely as she put her arm around him. With great sensitivity, she said, "Harry, the president is dead." Truman reflected for a brief moment before asking, "Eleanor, is there anything we can do for you?" Mrs. Roosevelt replied, "Harry, is there anything we can do for you? For you are the one in trouble now!"

Harry S Truman had assumed the presidency at a most critical time. World War II was coming to its end in Europe, but in Asia, Japan still thought she could win the war, and thousands of Americans were shedding their blood to prove otherwise. In places like Saipan, Guam, Manila, and Iwo Jima, U.S. losses were heartbreaking. While at Potsdam with Churchill, Stalin, and Clement Attlee, the British diplomat, on July 26, 1945, to iron out postwar settlements and to demand the surrender of Japan, President Truman was informed that the first atomic bomb test had been a success. In a carefully worded message, Truman warned the Japanese government that the "alternative" to their continued aggression "is complete and utter destruction." No reference was made to the atomic bomb. The man who did not mince words with diplomatic language would not tolerate the Japan situation any longer. Pearl Harbor's infamy would be reckoned with, and according to Truman's advisers the war would be shortened.

At the time military information assessed that the only U.S. alternative to the A bomb was a long, extended war with Japan, with an invasion not possible before a year; in the meantime, a mounting death toll could number near a million Allied troops. President Truman made the most momentous decision anyone would ever have to make. He sanctioned the dropping of two atomic bombs on Japan, one on the city of Hiroshima on August 6, 1945, and a second on the city of Nagasaki on August 9, 1945. More than two hundred thousand people were wiped out, and Japan hurried to the peace table. The war was over, and the nuclear age had arrived.

In 1948 Truman stunned the pollsters by defeating Thomas Dewey to gain a second term as president. On June 25, 1950, Communist planes flew across the Thirty-eighth Parallel into South Korea, and the Korean conflict began. Truman sent troops to the U.S. Far Eastern commander, General Douglas MacArthur, with orders to resist the North Korean Communist forces at all costs. In a policy dispute MacArthur was relieved of duty and "Give 'em hell Harry" suffered in the popularity polls. Truman couldn't care less. He was one of the most strong-willed, if not stubborn, of men. He spoke his mind, and one critic who said unflattering things about his daughter's singing heard from Truman in language that presidents never used—at least not in public. The unflappable Truman took daily two-mile walks with or without the Secret Service. Even after an assassination attempt, Truman still went about town seeing to the nation's business.

Once called a "roughneck ward politician," Truman talked and acted plainly. He called his wife, Bess, "the boss," liked to play the piano, and was a great baseball fan. The historic Truman Doctrine put the world on notice that the United States would defend her interests and her security when threatened directly or indirectly. After his presidency, Truman returned to his native Missouri.

JOSEPH STALIN

Last Day of Life: The Soviet dictator Joseph Stalin died on March 5, 1953.

Background: Much of the distrust of the Soviet Union began during the Stalin regime, and, ironically, when the Russian leader died on March 5, 1953, the Soviet account of his passing was viewed with suspicion. Stalin's daughter, Svetlana Alliluyeva, in her 1967 book *Twenty Letters to a Friend,* refutes Soviet accounts of her father's death.

According to *Pravda,* Russia's chief daily newspaper, and numerous Moscow radio accounts, Stalin, seventy-three, who had not been seen in the final months of his life due to illness, had died of a cerebral hemorrhage. The man who proved to be a skilled negotiator at the Yalta Conference in 1945 that enabled legitimate Russian expansion beyond its own frontiers and brought Communist governments to Poland, Hungary, Romania and Bulgaria, the man who in the 1930s had purged Russia of its old Bolsheviks, among them Leon Trotsky and the original members of the Russian triumvirate— Grigori Zinoviev and Lev Kamenev—died a disputed death.

If we accept his daughter's version of Stalin's death, which she witnessed, Joseph Stalin did not die at Moscow and did not slip away when his heart ceased to beat. According to his daughter, Stalin died in the small Russian hamlet of Kuntsevo, six miles from Moscow, in a cottage with medical people and Politburo members around his bed. His death was one of torment: Stalin spent hours gasping for breath. At the moment before his end came, it dawned on Stalin, a man who commonly liquidated his enemies, that indeed he might also be a victim of poisoning. Did Joseph Stalin suddenly come to the numbing, realization that *he* was being liquidated? The Russian dictator raised his failing left hand as if motioning toward the ceiling to call upon the Almighty in condemnation of some of those at his bed, his eyes wide, passing in accusation from one face to another. Shortly after, as Stalin groped for one last breath, he died.

Born at Gori, Georgia, in the Caucasus, Russia, on December 21, 1879, Joseph Stalin led a childhood life of crime that caused him to end up in Siberia several times. He came to power with Lenin and Trotsky during the Russian Revolution. Lenin did not trust him and intended to have him removed when death claimed him in 1924 before he got the chance. Trotsky hated Stalin. After Stalin forced Trotsky out of Russia, Stalin had him murdered in 1940.

With Lenin and Trotsky gone from the Russian scene, a power struggle brought Stalin his prize of dictatorship of Russia. No leader of Russia since Ivan the Terrible was crueler. Instituting new policies of industrialization and collectivization of agriculture, Stalin met opposition from some segments of Russian society. The dictator had those people crushed, murdering tens of millions by sending them to camps in Siberia, known as gulags, where they died of starvation and exposure to the extreme cold. Stalin's negotiation at the Yalta (1945) and Teheran (1943) conferences gained Russia dominance over Eastern Europe. No modern Russian was more feared than Joseph Stalin, a leading figure in what became known as the Cold War. Today Joseph Stalin epitomizes Russian tyranny.

DEVIL'S ISLAND

Last Day As Penal Colony: After one hundred years of existence, Devil's Island closed on August 22, 1953.

Background: Owned by France, the notorious lockup off the cost of French Guiana in South America was nicknamed the dry guillotine. From 1895 to 1899 it was the place of incarceration of Major Alfred Dreyfus, France's most famous political prisoner, who had been wrongly accused of selling French military secrets to Germany.

Devil's Island gets its name from the fact that the island was one of the most inhospitable places on earth. Founded in 1852, Ile de Diable was surrounded by a treacherous sea of massive waves and undercurrents—a sea inhabited by several species of sharks. Escapes were rare. The tropical climate spawned vicious malaria-carrying mosquitoes and the jungle island was infested with poisonous snakes. The treatment by the guards was so harsh that some prisoners never lived out their sentences. Though the penal colony was officially abolished in 1938, the onset of World War II delayed its actual closing for fifteen years.

The French would like to forget Ile de Diable, which became linked with the Dreyfus affair that exposed ineptness and corruption in the military. Dreyfus, hated for being a Jew, was deliberately sent to Devil's Island in the hope that he would never return. France liked to send its political prisoners, bandits, and murderers to Devil's Island because of its distance from their shores. One of the few prisoners successfully to escape Devil's Island was Henri Charriere, who sold butterflies while a fugitive. Charriere wrote the international bestseller *Papillon* (*papillon* means "butterfly"), banned in France, which added to the fame and legend of the hell on earth known as Devil's Island.

KOREAN WAR

Last Day: The Korean War ended in a stalemate on July 27, 1953.

Background: The Korean War began on June 25, 1950, when North Koreans invaded South Korea. Because the United States and South Korea were allies, U.S. President Truman on June 27, 1950, sent U.S. military warships and planes to the scene of the aggression in an effort to drive the invaders back from the Thirty-eighth Parallel which they had crossed. The North Koreans captured the South Korean capital city of Seoul on June 28; it was recaptured by South Korean and United States ground troops. Lieutenant General Walton Walker commanded U.S. troops; after Walker was killed in an automobile accident, Lieutenant General Matthew B. Ridgeway, took command. The United Nations troops were under the command of U.S. General Douglas MacArthur. When MacArthur wished to drive the Chinese forces supporting the North Koreans back into Manchuria and threatened Communist China with air and naval attack, which would have caused all-out war with China, President Truman removed him from all his Far East commands on April 11, 1951, and replaced him with General Ridgeway. North Korean soldiers killed: 316,579; Chinese soldiers killed: 422,612; United States soldiers killed: 37,904; United Nations Forces killed: approximately 4,521. Over 8,000 U.S. soldiers are still listed as missing in action.

GABRIELLE "COCO" CHANEL

Last Creation: In the spring of 1954, the fashion designer who came to be known as Coco Chanel introduced her collarless braid-trimmed cardigan jacket with a graceful skirt.

Background: Coco Chanel was world famous for her perfume, an expensive fragrance she named Chanel No. 5, (she believed five was her lucky number). Perhaps her best asset as a fashion designer was her understated simple elegance that also conveyed a sense of chic. The supreme French designer of the haute couture, she offered the world a glimpse of her designs on the fifth of each month in widely publicized fashion shows; Chanel was also famous for introducing women to short hair, costume jewelry, slim and straight suits without collars, and what became known and admired as the "little black dress."

Coco Chanel employed almost four thousand people. Her clothes were designed with both simplicity and function in mind. She literally moved fashion away from the complicated and inhibiting nineteenth-century styles that had lingered into the twentieth century. Even larger women could find comfort and ease in a Chanel design, a classic look that seemed to transcend time and conventions. Coco Chanel remained active until her death. Chanel No. 5 is still one of the world's best-selling perfumes, and it keeps Coco's name alive in the annals of fashion history. Marilyn Monroe claimed to have worn only Chanel No. 5 to bed.

PIUS X

Last Pope Canonized a Saint: Pope Pius X was canonized by the Roman Catholic Church on May 29, 1954.

ELLIS ISLAND

Last Day: Ellis Island functioned as a receiving station for immigrants until November 29, 1954. The next day the most famous immigration station in the world closed its gates. The reason: The outmoded facilities were too costly to operate as the dwindling flow of immigrants no longer arrived only by sea.

Background: Ellis Island, which lies beyond the Statue of Liberty in the upper bay of New York harbor, was the gateway to liberty, well-being, and the hope of a new life for millions coming to the New World. It had operated as an immigrant facility since before the Civil War. Immigrants arrived by steamer, often crowded into storage class, many disembarking with cardboard suitcases filled with possessions, clothes, and favorite photographs, while some immigrants came from Europe with nothing but the clothes on their backs. A ferry conveyed the future Americans to Ellis Island immigration depot, where overworked doctors processed as many as five thousand men, women, and children a day. The examinations were brief but thorough, with the doctors observing gaits and mannerisms; taking blood samples; checking eyes, mouth, tongues, and hands; and being particularly on the lookout for parasitic diseases, heart and respiratory ailments, and eye disorders. Linguists interviewed each immigrant, and public charges, criminals, prostitutes, the mentally ill, and anarchists were held in a detention center to await deportation.

Ellis Island was also known as the Isle of Tears, because of the many who were sent back to Europe, thus separating families. Today Ellis Island, consisting of some thirty-five buildings with their European neo-Renaissance spires looking out on New York harbor, is part of the Liberty National Monument, under the United States Interior Department since 1965. Actor Rudolph Valentino, physicist Albert Einstein, comedian Bob Hope, composer Irving Berlin, and radio and television pioneer David Sarnoff were some of the millions to pass through Ellis Island into the stream of American life, helping to shape its culture. Ellis Island is named after Samuel Ellis of New Jersey, a famous merchant who was once part owner of the island.

BAO DAI

Last Monarch of Vietnam: Emperor Bao Dai lost his throne in a national referendum that abolished the monarchy on October 23, 1955, giving way to a republic form of government.

Background: Bao Dai was proclaimed emperor of all Vietnam in 1949. When the southeast Asia nation was divided in 1954, his power remained in South Vietnam until the monarchy was abolished. Bao Dai was replaced by Ngo Dinh Diem as president. Diem died violently on November 1, 1963. Political instability gripped the nation and eventually led to the Vietnam War.

ANDREA DORIA

Last Day: On July 26, 1956, the *Andrea Doria* sank off the Nantucket Shoals, sixty miles off Nantucket Island, Massachusetts.

Background: Nearing the end of her voyage from Genoa, Italy, to New York, the beautiful 697-foot, 30,000-ton *Andrea Doria* on the night of July 25 observed another vessel on her radar screen. It was the Swedish-American *Stockholm,* which was alerted to the *Andrea Doria* when a pip signal began dotting her radar screen. The *Andrea Doria's* officers on the bridge, observing the *Stockholm* through a thin fog, were convinced the liners were in no danger of colliding, though they were passing dangerously within two miles of each other. Failure on the part of the *Andrea Doria's* officers to properly gauge the speed of the *Stockholm* would prove fatal. Packing a thrust of forty-five miles an hour, like a sudden terrible specter, the *Stockholm* was upon the *Andrea Doria,* shaking the Italian liner with battering-ram force. The *Stockholm*—a smaller vessel, but one whose bow had a reinforced ice-breaker—plowed into the *Andrea Doria's* hull, leaving a massive eighty-foot hole into which the sea rushed. The cry of distress signals sent the mighty *Ile de France,* which was in the vicinity, rushing to the stricken Italian's liner's aid.

The *Stockholm* managed to survive intact. A total of 1,706 passengers from the *Andrea Doria* were saved. Fifty-two persons perished, five of the deaths occurring on the *Stockholm.* After foundering throughout the night, at midmorning on July 26 the *Andrea Doria* began her descent, shortly settling to the depths of the sea, thirty-nine fathoms deep.

Twenty-eight years later, a salvage expedition underwritten at a cost of $2 million by Peter Gimbel and Elga Anderson in 1984 brought up one of two safes from the dead vessel. It was the bank safe; they had been unable to find the purser's safe. The safe was opened on national television on August 16, 1984; it contained bundles of Italian currency. The broadcast also included a film depicting the daring salvage expedition and exploring the "missing door" theory. Speculation had it that a water-tight steel door leading to the ship's generator room had been negligently removed, allowing the rushing sea water to flood the generator, thus shutting down the *Andrea Doria*'s power and leaving her without functioning pumps, which caused her demise. The salvage team headed by Ted Hess discovered what caused the *Andrea Doria*'s end. The *Stockholm*'s bow had plunged into the generator room flooding the generators seconds after making contact with the hull of the liner.

MUHAMMAD VIII, AL-AMIN

Last Monarch of Tunis: King Muhammad VIII al-Amin, the bey, was deposed as ruler of Tunis (now Tunisia) on July 25, 1957, when by a vote of the constituent assembly, the nation at the northwest bulge of Africa became a republic, under the presidency of Habib Bourguiba. Muhammad VIII was the last of the Hussein Dynasty of beys established almost three centuries before in 1705. He died in 1962.

EBBETS FIELD

Last World Series: In the last series at Ebbets Field, home of the Brooklyn Dodgers, the New York Yankees took the championship in the seventh game on October 10, 1956. That was also Dodger Jackie Robinson's last game in the major leagues.

Background: The field was named after Hall of Famer Charles Ebbets, owner of the Dodgers (then called the Trolley Dodgers) at the turn of the century; he had been a pioneer in the fight for Sunday games. Ebbets Field welcomed the first black player in modern major league history when on April 15, 1947, Jackie Roosevelt Robinson of the Dodgers took his place at second base in a game against the Boston Braves. It was also the site of the first color television broadcast of a baseball game on August 11, 1951. The signs around the stadium advertised Schaefer Beer and Old Gold Cigarettes. A suit sign in left field, if hit by a batsman, was good for a free suit. Ebbets Field has historically become known as the home of "The Boys of Summer"—Roy Campanella, Jackie Robinson, Pee Wee Reese, Gil Hodges, Billy Cox, Don Newcombe, Carl Erskine, Glem Labine, Duke Snider, Carl Furillo, Preacher Roe, Joe Black, and others. In 1957 team owner Walter O'Malley, although making money from devoted Flatbush fans, nevertheless moved the team to greener pastures in Los Angeles.

Last Home Run: The Dodgers Duke Snider hammered the last homer in Ebbets Field off Philadelphia Phillies pitcher Robin Roberts on September 24, 1957.

Last Game: On September 26, 1957, the Brooklyn Dodgers beat the Pittsburgh Pirates 2–0. Attendance: 6,702 fans.

POLO GROUNDS

Last Giants Game: The home team New York Giants lost to the Pittsburgh Pirates 9–1 on September 29, 1957.

Background: Home of baseball's New York Giants, the Polo Grounds is famous for Bobby Thomson's "Shot Heard 'Round the World" on October 3, 1951, when, in a game against the Brooklyn Dodgers, Thomson unloaded off a Ralph Branca pitch for a home run to win the pennant. At the Polo Grounds on August 16, 1920, pitcher Carl Mays of the New York Yankees (Yanks played games at Polo Grounds until Yankee Stadium was built) fatally beaned Ray Chapman of the Cleveland Indians, who died of his injuries marking the first and only time in major league history that a player was killed as a result of a game (batting helmets were not used then).

On July 10, 1934, at the All-Star Game, Carl Hubbell struck out five batters in a row: Babe Ruth, Lou Gehrig, Jimmie Foxx, Al Simmons, and Joe Cronin—all now in baseball's Hall of Fame. Babe Ruth hit 69 of his 714 home runs at the Polo Grounds, the last on September 5, 1922, off pitcher Herb Pennock of the Boston Red Sox. There on September 29, 1954, Willie Mays of the Giants made a circus catch of a thunderous drive off the bat of Vic Wertz of the Cleveland Indians in the last World Series at the Polo Grounds. Famous boxing matches at the Polo Grounds include Rocky Marciano over Roland LaStarza in round eleven on September 24, 1953, and Floyd Patterson successfully defending his world crown against Hurricane Jackson in round ten via a knockout on July 29, 1957. The New York Giants moved to San Francisco for the 1958 season. The New York Mets used the field during the 1962 and 1963 seasons. The stadium was torn down April 10, 1964.

FAISAL II

Last Monarch of Iraq: King Faisal II was assassinated on July 14, 1958, along with his infant son, in a coup masterminded by General Abdul Karem Kassim.

Background: Born on May 2, 1935, Faisal became king upon the death of his father in an automobile accident on April 4, 1939. Faisal was known for his pro-Western leanings. After his death at age twenty-three, Iraq was proclaimed a republic.

ILE DE FRANCE

Last Voyage: On November 18, 1958, the luxurious *Ile de France* sailed from New York to France.

Background: Famous for coming to the aid of the stricken *Andrea Doria,* the three-funnel *Ile de France* first took to the seas in 1926. Seized by Great Britain during World War II to prevent her from sailing for the Nazis, she served the British as a troop carrier. She was known for her unusually brilliant lights (trademark of the

French line vessels), a characteristic that proved to be the good fortune of the passengers of the *Andrea Doria*. She died in the scrapyards of Japan in 1961, but not before starring in the film *The Last Voyage,* with Robert Stack and Dorothy Malone—which upset her former French owners. She is remembered for providing the consummate in ocean-liner luxury.

FRANK LLOYD WRIGHT

Last Day of Life: Architect Frank Lloyd Wright succumbed to a heart attack while hospitalized for intestinal blockage, on April 9, 1959, in Phoenix, Arizona, at age ninety-two.

Background: One of the great architects of the twentieth century, Wright created architecture that appeared to grow out of its foundations, rather than looking as if it had been built by human hands. Detesting the stone and steel look, he created designs that were said to have the "organic look." Frank Lloyd Wright liked to be in tune with nature, designing interiors that seemed to be an extension of the natural environment that made up a property. He also detested structures that looked like boxes and equated them with coffins. The Grady Gammage Memorial Auditorium of Arizona State University at Tempe, Arizona, 1959, was Wright's last nonresidential design. The last residence he designed was the Norman Lykes residence in Phoenix, Arizona, also in 1959. Wright's final creation was a beautiful enclosed garden for his wife at Taliesin Spring Green, Wisconsin, in 1959.

Among Frank Lloyd Wright's most famous structures are the Guggenheim Museum in New York City and the Larkin Building in Buffalo, New York. The protagonist of the novel *The Fountainhead* by Ayn Rand is believed to be modeled on Frank Lloyd Wright.

MEYER LANSKY

Last Crime: It has been substantiated that Meyer Lansky ordered the murder of gangster Little Augie Carfano on September 25, 1959, in New York City.

Background: Born of Jewish parents, Lansky at age sixteen had a chance meeting with Bugsy Siegel that resulted in a lifelong friendship. Lansky defended Bugsy in a dispute with a violent pimp. The pimp, it turned out, was Charles "Lucky" Luciano, who was to become one of the most powerful mobsters of the twentieth century. He remembered Lansky, who had felled him with a monkey wrench. Luciano had heard that Lansky maintained a successful gang of enforcers and ran just as successful crap games. Sicilian mobster Luciano enlisted Lansky in his criminal ventures that added to the violence of the Roaring Twenties.

Luciano organized a "combination," or syndicate, of brainy gangsters who pooled their ill-gotten resources to underwrite such rackets as gambling, prostitution, bootlegging, and selling stolen furs and cars. He gave Lansky a major role in his scheme by placing him on the board of the syndicate. The syndicate recruited well-paid hired killers to exterminate rival gang members and betrayers of the syndicate. This gave rise to the infamous Murder Incorporated.

The syndicate, run by Lansky from New York, had dealings with the most powerful gangland figures of the day—Al Capone, Louis "Lepke" Buchalter, Albert Anastasia, Frank Costello, and others. Lansky's operations extended to Cuba, where his syndicate operated gambling casinos with the blessing of dictator Fulgencio Batista, who sliced off a sizable chunk of the annual take.

Tough, brutal, but loyal to the syndicate, Lansky, adhering to the will of Lucky Luciano, ordered the murder of many, including his bosom buddy Bugsy Siegel, for welching on the syndicate to the tune of millions. Through the 1940s and 1950s Lansky grew more powerful, engineering a parole for syndicate head Luciano after he was jailed for criminal activities; by the 1960s Lansky's empire extended far and near, and the millions he made were salted away in Swiss numbered accounts. By then Lansky had been involved in illicit drugs, pornography, extortion and money laundering.

In 1970 Lansky escaped to Israel, fearing an indictment for income tax evasion. He was eventually returned to the United States and convicted of income tax evasion, but remained free on appeals. Meyer Lansky's last years were filled with physical pain as he suffered from cancer. Though he was a millionaire many times over, he was remembered as a modest spender and for his $1 tips to waiters. The man with so much blood on his hands, Meyer Lansky was silenced by lung cancer forever.

EBBETS FIELD

Last Day: Ebbets Field was demolished on February 23, 1960, to make way for an apartment building.

DWIGHT DAVID EISENHOWER

(Thirty-fourth President of the United States)

Last Day in Office: January 20, 1961, after two terms.

Background: Eisenhower loved to play golf and liked to paint. A great army general, he was loyal to his friends, prayerful, humble, and exceptionally kind to soldiers. He sent unknown sums of money to down-and-out veterans and their families.

MICHAEL ROCKEFELLER

Last Seen: Michael Rockefeller disappeared on November 18, 1961, on a river in New Guinea.

Background: While on an expedition in New Guinea to find the Asmat tribe, the twenty-three-year-old son of Nelson Rockefeller, then New York governor, was caught in a sudden storm that caused his dugout canoe to capsize as he was guided along the New Guinea coast. Two Papuan guides escaped to shore while Rockefeller and senior anthropologist Dr. René Wassink chose to stay with the stricken craft and equipment. Wassink watched young Rockefeller swim off until, "I could only see three dots—his head and the two red gallon cans. Then he disappeared across my horizon." Notified in New York, Governor Rockefeller went to New Guinea and organized search parties, but his son was never found.

LIBERTE

Last Day: The luxury liner *Liberte* met her demise on December 30, 1961, at an Italian scrapyard.

Background: Remembered for exceptional cuisine, the *Liberte* had a menu that filled the pages of *Holiday* magazine. Formerly owned by Germany and known as the *Europa,* she was awarded to France as part of World War II indemnities. The *Liberte* had a complement of 160 chefs, and she promised her passengers would gain weight—at least a pound a day—and indeed they did, with all foods prepared with French pomp and culinary grandeur. The *Liberte* had seven massive decks and the unusual design of a bulbous bow, built for speed (twenty-four knots). Indeed, she won a Blue Ribbon for speed. She was rammed by a stricken vessel in her home port, but survived to enjoy a splendid sea career. Her maiden voyage as a luxury liner was in 1950.

IMAM MANSUR BILLAH MUHAMMAD

Last Monarch of Yemen: The former crown prince, Imam Mansur Billah Muhammad, was deposed in 1962, after only recently succeeding his father, Imam Ahmed, who had died. Yemen is now a People's Democratic Republic.

CHARLES "LUCKY" LUCIANO

Last Day of Life: Lucky Luciano died on January 26, 1962.

Background: Luciano arrived in his limousine at the Capodichino Airport in Naples to greet film producer Martin Gosh, who had flown from the United States to discuss a possible movie on Luciano's life. Luciano was walking across the runway to meet the producer, his arm outstretched for a handshake, smiling happily, when suddenly his smile turned to an agonized grimace as he grabbed his shirtfront and fell to the pavement, dead from a heart attack on January 26, 1962. Born Salvatore Lucania in a small Sicilian hamlet of Lercara Friddi in 1896, he was sixty-six years old.

ALCATRAZ PRISON

Last Day: The federal prison located in San Francisco Bay and known as The Rock was closed on March 20, 1963. Reason: It was outmoded.

Background: The famous island prison that received its name from the Spanish word for pelican was the home of Al Capone, Machine Gun Kelly, Baby Face Nelson, and Robert Stroud—the Birdman of Alcatraz. Alcatraz Prison began as a military fortification and penitentiary in 1858. In 1934 the Rock became a federal maximum-security prison. It was said to be escape-proof because of its location in a four-mile choppy stretch of bay, waters known for vicious currents. No convict is believed to have successfully completed the four-mile swim from Alcatraz island to freedom. Today Alcatraz is a tourist attraction, a part of the Golden Gate National Recreation Area.

JOHN FITZGERALD KENNEDY
(Thirty-fifth President of the United States)

Last Day of Life: John F. Kennedy was assassinated on November 22, 1963, during his first term as president.

Background: President Kennedy went to Dallas, Texas on what was described as a fence-mending mission, a trip to unite disputing Democrats unhappy with the president's civil rights stand. President Kennedy needed their support for his anticipated run for reelection in 1964.

Upon landing at Love Airfield, Dallas, at 11:38 A.M. the president was received warmly by the people of Texas. His wife, Jacqueline Bouvier Kennedy, was presented with a bouquet of red roses. It was a bright sunny morning, not even crisp, and a great mass of people thronged the airport. Making himself comfortable in an open-air limousine, waving to the screaming crowds, the President and his wife were joined by Texas Governor John Connally and his wife. The presidential motorcade began to move toward downtown Dallas where Kennedy was to attend a reception and make a speech. It was a jubilant ride, with happy and goodhearted Texans extending a warm welcome—taking pictures, waving, blowing kisses, and raising their little tots to the president.

Between 12:28 and 12:30 P.M. the motorcade progressed just past Houston to Elm Street and was moving southwest past Dealey Plaza when shots sounded. The shots at first were thought to be automobile backfire. The president's limousine, moving at eleven miles an hour, kept that speed. Shock and disbelief seized Mrs. Kennedy at her husband's last words: "My God, I've been hit," those words uttered as a rifle bullet pierced the young president's neck, clearing his body to wound Governor Connally. The stricken president lurched forward as another bullet tore away the right side of his skull. It seemed that only Mrs. Kennedy witnessed the horror, and only when the hysterical First Lady stood up in the vehicle, her dress soaked with blood, and began to climb onto the car trunk did others recognize the tragedy.

The limousine roared forth to Parklane Memorial Hospital, arriving at emergency room one, where doctors knew it was too late to save the president, and attempts to revive him failed. A Roman Catholic priest, Father Oscar L. Huber, hurried to the unconscious president, administering the sacrament of Extreme Unction. At 1 o'clock Eastern Standard Time, President John F. Kennedy was pronounced dead.

He was killed by an assassin named Lee Harvey Oswald, using a high-powered World War II Italian-made Mannlicher Carcano 6.5-mm rifle. The second of three bullets fired by Oswald from the sixth floor of the Texas School Book Depository—the bullet that struck Kennedy's head—was the fatal bullet. Ironically, the School Book Depository had in its warehouse many new books on the young president, "the president of a thousand days."

Born in Brookline, Massachusetts, on May 29, 1917, Kennedy was forty-six years old. President Kennedy told Americans: "Ask not what your country can do for you; ask what you can do for your country."

No president of the United States was as suave, affable and handsome as John Fitzgerald Kennedy. Born into wealth, he loved the arts, literature, and sports and was a fine orator. His administration's New Frontier program gave rise to the Peace Corps, took America into the era of space exploration and improved the plight of the nation's poor. Unfortunately, the young president's administration was also marked by such sorrows as a failed invasion of Cuba at the Bay of Pigs, and a congress that would not pass his domestic programs. However, one moment in Kennedy's presidency stands as a monument to courage in the face of adversity—the moment when he blocked the Soviet Union as it sought to stockpile missiles in Cuba only ninety miles from the Florida coast. The Russians backed down, thus avoiding an all out war in what became known as the Cuban Missile Crisis.

President Kennedy was no King Arthur of Camelot; indeed he had feet of clay. But his brief presidency of a thousand days is still perceived as a cherished moment in American history. His first lady was the charming Jacquline Bouvier Kennedy who gave him a son and a daughter. Americans will always remember John F. Kennedy as simply J.F.K., a man with a great sense of humor and style.

Gravesite: Arlington National Cemetery, Arlington, Virginia.

RONALD REAGAN
(Fortieth President of the United States)

Last Film: Before becoming president, Reagan was an actor. His last movie was *The Killers* in 1964, a remake of the 1946 classic.

HERBERT CLARK HOOVER
(Thirty-first President of the United States)

Last Day of Life: Herbert Hoover died on October 20, 1964.

Background: Spending his last years in New York City at the Waldorf Towers, Herbert Hoover in mid-October of 1964 succumbed to bleeding in his gastrointestinal tract. All efforts to stem the hemorrhaging failed, and on the morning of October 20, 1964, in his suite, the former chief executive passed away. Born August 10, 1874, in West Branch, Iowa, he was ninety years old.

Gravesite: Herbert Hoover Historic Site, West Branch, Iowa.

WINSTON CHURCHILL

Last Day of Life: British statesman, author, and prime minister Winston Churchill died on January 24, 1965.

Background: Great Britain's most notable prime minister was not himself in his final years. In retirement, though still a member of Parliament, he displayed little of the energy and resoucefulness that marked his service during the war years. Issues of the day did not stir him and he read less. His wife, Lady Churchill, was ever at his side, but his zest for life was gone; old age was upon the man Britain had come to know as Winnie. He suffered a stroke on January 12, 1965, and was confined to his bed at his home in Hyde Park Gate, England. On January 24, 1965, with his wife and daughter Mary at his bedside, the man who won the hearts of both Britons and Americans with his zeal and good nature died peacefully.

Of all British politicians, none has gained the affection and respect accorded Winston Churchill, a brilliant war leader who was the first to signal to the world the dangers of Nazism. A former soldier who was educated at Sandhurst, he was elected to the British Parliament in 1900 as a Conservative and served as first lord of the admiralty from 1911 to 1915. Upon the ouster of Prime Minister Neville Chamberlain's government as a result of Chamberlain's handling of negotiations with Nazi Germany's Hitler in a quest for peace, Winston Churchill became prime minister in 1940. Along with President Roosevelt, he was one of the principal signers of the important Atlantic Charter, a document designed to spread peace and democracy, pledging a "permanent system of general security" to be established after the war; hence, the seeds of the United Nations were sown.

Churchill's most historic statements concerned his "iron curtain" statement in which he predicted an iron curtain would fall across Europe, separating the free nations from those whose people were under the yoke of the USSR. After the war, Churchill was out of power for some five years before returning as prime minister in 1951 and retiring in 1955. He served as an active member of the British Parliament until 1964. Winston Churchill was a profound figure on the world stage, a lover of peace, and a statesman with vision and courage.

HARVARD UNIVERSITY

Last Year of All-Male Students: Harvard was an all-male bastion through 1966.

Background: Founded in 1636 as a university for men, Harvard admitted its first female student in the autumn of 1967. Women had previously attended the university's summer program.

QUEEN ELIZABETH I

Last Voyage: On May 8, 1967, her captain, while at sea on a trip to New York City, opened a sealed letter informing him of the *Queen*'s retirement.

Background: Built in 1940—though her maiden voyage was not taken until 1946—the *Queen Elizabeth I* (often called *QEI*) was the world's longest ship until nosed out by the *France* (in 1962). The *Queen Elizabeth I* represented the finest in ocean-liner luxury, with plush suites and Russian caviar for her discriminating passengers. A first-class ticket cost $3,000. During World War II she was secretly battle-fitted. A German submarine spotted the pride of Great Britain on the high seas, but for some unexplained reason, the submarine commander spared the *Queen*. The *Queen Elizabeth I* completed more than nine hundred Atlantic crossings. She was sold to the city of Fort Lauderdale, Florida, to become a tourist attraction, then was resold to an Asian merchant in Hong Kong. On January 10, 1972, the *Queen Elizabeth I* caught fire and capsized while she sat at dockside in Fort Lauderdale, Florida.

QUEEN MARY

Last Voyage: On September 22, 1967, the *Queen Mary* sailed from New York to Southampton, England.

Background: Built by John Brown & Company, Ltd. in May 1936, the *Queen Mary* had a speed of thirty-two knots and was the winner of a Blue Ribbon. The old slogan, "Getting there is half the fun," was certainly true in the case of the *Queen Mary*. She was a floating palace, gracious with regal appointments. A first-class ticket from England to New York cost $3,000. She had swimming pools, tennis courts, movies, dancing halls, the finest food in sea travel, and the most modern equipment and design, and if her appetite for oil had not been so ravenous, she would still be reigning as queen of the world's ocean liners—a superliner indeed. The only ship that touched her was the *United States*. So proud were her owners that they suppressed the fact that the *Queen Mary* had rammed the little cruiser the *Curacoa*, a convoy ship charged with protecting the mighty *Queen* in dangerous Irish waters. She was losing $3 million a year. On August 18, 1967 the highest bidder, a California concern, won her for a price of $3,450,000. Today the former *Queen Mary* of the Cunard Line holds court at Pier J in Long Beach, California, where she reigns as a floating museum.

CONSTANTINE II

Last Monarch of Greece: King Constantine II (also known as Constantine XIII) was dethroned December 14, 1967, when a military junta of generals seized political power. A coup by the deposed king to regain power failed, and

Constantine II with his family went into exile. In 1973
Greece became a republic.

VINCE LOMBARDI

Last Game as Green Bay Packers Coach: Football coach
Vince Lombardi led the Packers to a victory over the
Oakland Raiders in Super Bowl II, 33–14, on January 16,
1968, at Super Bowl Stadium in Florida. He then retired
temporarily before taking over as Washington Redskins
coach in 1969.

Background: Born in New York City in 1913, Vince
Lombardi was a graduate of Fordham University. He
became head football coach of Fordham from 1939
through 1946, and then West Point Military Academy
football coach from 1949 though 1953. His college
football years were so successful that he went on to
coach pro football. Lombardi became head coach of
the New York Giants from 1954 through 1958. However, it was not until he took over the Green Bay
Packers that he found fame that made him a national celebrity and took him to professional football's
Hall of Fame. He guided the Packers to six conference titles, five national championships, and two Super Bowls, numbers I and II. When he left the
coaching helm, Green Bay's fortunes sank. He is remembered for saying, "Winning isn't everything, but
wanting to win is," which has generally been mis-
quoted as "Winning isn't everything, it's the only
thing."

MARTIN LUTHER KING, JR.

Last Day of Life: Civil rights leader Martin Luther King, Jr.,
was assassinated on April 4, 1968.

Background: Martin Luther King, Jr., first attracted the attention of a wide majority of Americans with his march on
Washington, D.C., in 1963. He espoused a nonviolent
philosophy. King's passionate interest in equal rights for

black people in a land that was supposed to guarantee such rights by its Constitution gained the black leader many admirers and some enemies. Few Americans faced as much adversity as King: imprisonment, beatings by police and white toughs, little cooperation from U.S. Justice Department officials. King's poignant "I have a dream" speech in 1963, in which he expressed his impassioned goals, touched the hearts and consciences of the world, and in 1964 he was awarded the Nobel Peace Prize.

An American Baptist clergyman and leader of the Southern Christian Leadership Conference, King in 1968 turned his attention to the Vietnam War, advocating a peaceful withdrawal. Few issues divided Americans more than Vietnam, and King's stance was partly responsible for swaying public opinion against the war. In that same year King wept after a stormy march in Memphis, Tennessee, in support of sanitation employees, that resulted in confrontations between marchers and police, with one black youth losing his life. Less than one month later the civil rights leader was in Memphis for the last time.

Before his fortieth birthday, King was staying at the Lorraine Motel on Mulberry Street in Memphis, on April 4, 1968. In early evening he was preparing to dine with other members of the Southern Christian Leadership Conference at a member's home. Leaving his room, King had only to put on a jacket and lock his room door when he walked a few feet to a tier railing to suggest to associates in rooms below the music program for the dinner-prayer meeting. Standing at the railing, King smiled as he called down, "Ben [Ben Branch], make sure you play 'Precious Lord, Take My Hand.' Play it real pretty for me." They were the last words he would ever speak, for with a sudden sharp noise, a powerful rifle bullet smashed through his face, killing him instantly. The bullet came from across the street where James Earl Ray had committed the murder with a hunting rifle. He had fired the rifle from a rooming house. Born in Atlanta, Georgia, on January 15, 1929, King was thirty-nine years old.

ROBERT FRANCIS KENNEDY

Last Day of Life: Presidential hopeful Robert F. Kennedy was felled by an assassin's bullet on June 6, 1968.

Background: The brother of John F. Kennedy, Robert, the former U.S. Attorney General and the senator from New York, was riding a crest of popularity that might have given him the presidency of the United States. Bobby had the Kennedy charm, political wisdom, and enemies.

One of his enemies had the mind of an assassin. He was a self-destructive fanatic who despised the presidential candidate for his pro-Israel stance, which included giving arms to the Jewish state. The man's name was Sirhan Bishara Sirhan, age twenty-four. His home was in Jerusalem and he had been in the United States for some ten years. Sirhan managed to clear a lax security check and place himself within feet of Kennedy at approximately 12:15 A.M. at the Ambassador Hotel in Los Angeles, California. It was June 5, 1968. Kennedy had just delivered a speech celebrating his victory in the California primary, crucial to his nomination as the Democratic presidential candidate. Mobbed by well-wishers as he was being led through the pantry of the hotel, Kennedy graciously attempted to shake all the extended hands of congratulations. Suddenly, amid the jubilation, three sharp cracks sounded from behind Kennedy—gunfire from a .22-caliber Iver-Johnson revolver. Kennedy sank from the throng; as panic ensued, the gunman fired another five shots before Roosevelt Grier, a strapping six-foot-tall ex-pro-football player, wrestled the gun from the assassin's hand. The pantry was stifling as attempts were made to clear the area of people to allow Kennedy some air. As a bullet wound behind Kennedy's right ear spilled blood, a rosary was placed in his failing hands.

Kennedy was rushed to Good Samaritan Hospital in Los Angeles, where a team of surgeons performed three operations. The next day, June 6, 1968, at 1:44 A.M., Robert F. Kennedy was pronounced dead, less than five years after his brother John F. Kennedy had also been assassinated, and two months after the assassination of Martin Luther King, Jr. Robert F. Kennedy was forty-two years old.

SILVER CERTIFICATE

Last Time As Part of U.S. Currency Standard: June 24, 1968, was the last day the U.S. Treasury Department redeemed the silver certificates for silver bars.

LYNDON BAINES JOHNSON
(Thirty-sixth President of the United States)

Last Day in Office: January 20, 1969, after more than one term. Johnson became the thirty-sixth president upon the assassination of John F. Kennedy.

Background: The thirty-sixth president of the United States was thrust into the nation's highest office on November 22, 1963, in the presidential airplane, Air Force One, upon the death of John F. Kennedy. He liked to be surrounded by the public and was one of the most accessible of men, who gave a hearty handshake and a warm bear hug to visitors. He lacked drawing room manners and certainly spoke his mind. He had a huge appetite and loved puddings and barbecued ribs.

DWIGHT DAVID EISENHOWER
(Thirty-fourth President of the United States)

Last Day of Life: Dwight Eisenhower died on March 28, 1969.

Background: The former U.S. Army general and supreme commander of Allied forces in World War II in Europe, one of America's favorite presidents, had been bothered by various illnesses connected to heart disease even before his first term as the thirty-fourth United States president. He was in and out of Walter Reed Hospital in Washington, D.C. While he was in the hospital during his final months of life, visitors from around the world came to see the man whose campaign slogan was "I Like Ike." Songs from his favorite musical, *The Sound of Music,* were performed on the hospital lawn, children called to the hospital window, mail carriers delivered hundreds of sacks of letters and cards from well-wishers, and doctors issued daily news briefings on Ike's progress. Though his death was expected, the nation was no less saddened when it occurred.

In one of his last alert moments, Ike spoke his last words: "I've always loved my wife, I've always loved my children, I've always loved my grandchildren, and I've always loved my country." Hours later, on March 28, 1969, Dwight David Eisenhower closed his eyes and died. Born in Denison, Texas, on October 14, 1890, he was seventy-eight years old.

Gravesite: Eisenhower Center, Abilene, Kansas.

IDRIS I

Last Monarch of Libya: King Idris I was deposed in a bloodless coup d'etat on September 1, 1969.

Background: King Idris I came to power as king in 1951. He resides in exile in Egypt. Formally known officially as Libya Arab Republic, his country is now the People's Socialist Libya Arab Republic.

UNITED STATES

Last Voyage: The *United States* sailed from Bremerhaven, Germany, and Southampton, England, to New York on November 1, 1969.

Background: In truth, the ocean liner *United States* had few equals. Built at an unheard-of cost of $75 million, she made her maiden voyage from New York to Le Havre, France, and Southampton, England, on July 3, 1952. Her interiors, from draperies to furniture to carpeting, were fireproof. The *United States* had seven decks

and raced at a top speed of thirty-six knots, good enough
to defeat the *Queen Mary* to capture the prestigious Blue
Ribbon, making her the fastest ocean liner in the world.
The *United States* had the finest appointments and ex-
terior regal looks. In the sweltering heat that can sometimes prevail in the Atlantic, the *United States* was amply
cooled with gales of marvelous air-conditioning to make
her almost three thousand passengers most comfortable
as they dined on the world's most sumptuous cuisine,
whose menus were often featured in *Holiday* magazine.
But she was losing $4 million to $5 million a year, and
the federal government grew tired of underwriting her
losses. Still, the *United States* ocean liner had no equals
when it came to stamina. A giant upon the seas, she was
a sea Hercules indeed.

VINCE LOMBARDI

Last Game: As coach of the Washington Redskins, Lombardi saw his team lose to the Dallas Cowboys at Dallas
on December 21, 1969 by the score of 20–10.

WILLIE SUTTON

Last Day in Prison: On Christmas Eve, 1969, Willie Sutton
was released from Attica Prison in upstate New York for
good behavior and due to illness. Sutton suffered from
emphysema.

VINCE LOMBARDI

Last Day of Life: Football coach Vince Lombardi died of
cancer on September 3, 1970.

GABRIELLE "COCO" CHANEL

Last Day of Life: On January 10, 1971, at the Ritz Hotel in
Paris, France, fashion designer Coco Chanel died from
natural causes. She was eighty-seven years old.

D. B. COOPER

Last Seen: Skyjacker D. B. Cooper parachuted from a Northwest Airlines 727 jet, Flight 305, on November 25, 1971.

Background: A skyjacker who called himself Dan Cooper and became known to the public as D.B. Cooper bailed out of the jet somewhere over the southwest part of Washington state with $200,000 and four parachutes he had demanded. The mysterious Dan Cooper, who was tall and dark and appeared to be in his forties, claimed to have a bomb in a briefcase set to explode unless he was flown to Mexico and given $200,000 and the four parachutes. He has since become a cult figure—Americans wear D. B. Cooper T-shirts and songwriters have created ballads about him.

An immediate search of the southwest wilderness of Washington state proved negative. The feeling among law officials is that the man descended unsuccessfully to his death from what was a bailout of ten thousand feet into dense forest. Law enforcement officials are certain that Dan Cooper was not the man's real name. The public came to call the skyjacker D. B. Cooper because the FBI thought the name Dan Cooper on the plane passenger list might be an alias for a known criminal named D. B. Cooper. That D. B. Cooper was in prison at the time of the 727 skyjacking.

Nine years after the Dan Cooper skyjacking, an eight-year-old boy on an outing with his parents found a soiled packet of $20 bills near the Columbia River, money the FBI agents identified as having been given to the mysterious Dan Cooper. An exhaustive search of the region by the federal authorities did not turn up any other traces of the skyjacker. With the eruption of Mount St. Helens in May 1980, which totally transformed the region, any possible evidence is certainly gone. Police believe Dan Cooper is dead, but they have no proof. The case remains open.

HARRY S TRUMAN

(Thirty-third President of the United States)

Last Day of Life: Harry S Truman died on December 26, 1972.

Background: Truman was hospitalized in Kansas City, Missouri, on December 5, 1972, suffering from hardening of the arteries and lung congestion. His condition weakened, and yet as Christmas approached, the sounds and sights of the season seemed to prolong the former president's life. His wife, Bess, and daughter, Margaret, were always nearby. Christmas came and went, and on the morning of December 26 at 7:50 A.M. Harry S Truman's heart gave out. Born in Lamar, Missouri, on May 8, 1884, he was eighty-eight years old.

Gravesite: Harry S Truman Memorial Library, Independence, Missouri.

LYNDON BAINES JOHNSON
(Thirty-sixth President of the United States).

Last Day of Life: Lyndon Johnson died on January 22, 1973.

Background: Even when he was not feeling well, Lyndon Johnson was busy on his ranch, writing and receiving visitors. He was the most public of presidents, yet his last moments were spent alone, without his kind, adoring wife, Lady Bird, and their two daughters. The day was January 22, 1973, at LBJ Ranch in Texas. A phone rang at the Secret Service quarters and was picked up by an agent. Lyndon Johnson urgently requested to speak to the head of the Secret Service detail. The man in charge was away, so Johnson asked the agent responding to his call to come quickly to his bedroom. The agent rushed to the president's bedroom, where he saw Johnson lying near his bed. He tried to take the president's pulse, but all life signs were gone. At 3:50 in the afternoon Lyndon Baines Johnson was pronounced dead. He had died of a heart attack. Born near Stonewall, Texas, on August 27, 1908, he was sixty-four years old.

Gravesite: LBJ Ranch, Stonewall, Texas.

VIETNAM WAR

Last Day: The Vietnam War ended on January 27, 1973, when the cease-fire agreement was signed in Paris, France by Secretary of State William P. Rogers for the United States and by representatives of North Vietnam, South Vietnam, and the Vietcong.

Background: Major United States involvement in the Vietnam War began on August 7, 1964, when the United States Senate passed the Gulf of Tonkin Resolution in response to an incident in which North Vietnamese P.T. boats attacked the U.S. destroyer *Maddox* on August 2, 1964. The Gulf of Tonkin Resolution gave President Lyndon Johnson unlimited military power to assist any nation in its defense under the Southeast Asia Collective Defense Treaty. The longest war to involve American soldiers cost 46,160 U.S. troops, with another 10,320 perishing in enemy prisons and many U.S. soldiers still unaccounted for. The war divided Americans, with "hawks" seeking a military solution to the war and "doves" seeking an unconditional and total withdrawal of American forces from Vietnam. American soldiers returning to the United States after the war found protests instead of parades and a struggle to win honor and fair recompense from Americans.

MOHAMMAD ZAHIR SHAH

Last Monarch of Afghanistan: King Mohammad Zahir Shah was deposed in a coup on July 17, 1973. A republic was declared.

Background: After the king was deposed, Mohammed Daud, former prime minister, became president and prime minister. Daud died in a subsequent coup, April 27, 1978. Afghanistan was taken over by the Soviets on December 27, 1980; the last day of Soviet military occupation was February 15, 1989.

RICHARD MILHOUS NIXON
(Thirty-seventh President of the United States)

Last Day in Office: August 9, 1974, during his second term.

Background: Richard Nixon resigned in the face of the Watergate scandal, the first U.S. president to do so. The first U.S. president to visit China, Nixon also visited Russia, improving relations with both of these superpowers. Both Nixon and Vice President Spiro Agnew left office in disgrace—Nixon because of the Watergate scandal, and Agnew due to an earlier scandal. Richard Nixon is remembered for his "Checkers speech" (1952), in which he exonerated himself on television before a national audience after charges that he had taken slush-fund money. But he did admit receiving a little dog (named Checkers by his children), which his daughters loved, and therefore, no matter what people thought, he kept the dog. He won the nation's heart. On another occasion, after losing a race for the governership of California (1962), Nixon, before the press, chided the reporters, saying "You won't have Dick Nixon to kick around because gentlemen, this is my last press conference."

He ended his last presidential speech to the nation, on August 8, 1974, announcing the resignation, with the words: "To have served in this office is to have felt a very personal sense of kinship with each and every American. In leaving it, I do so with this prayer: May God's grace be with you in all the years ahead."

FRANCE

Last Voyage: On September 5, 1974, the *France* sailed from New York to Southampton, England.

Background: The third ship built by France to bear the nation's name, the *France* was the French lines flagship. She sailed on her maiden voyage on February 3, 1962, from Le Havre, France, and Southampton, England, to New York. She was the world's longest ocean liner with dimensions of 1,035 feet by 111 feet. The *France* had seven massive decks, an excellent speed of thirty-two knots, and the ability to accommodate five hundred passengers in first class and fifteen hundred passengers in tourist class. When the *Queen Elizabeth I* went out of service in 1967, the *France* became the largest ocean liner on the seas.

HAILE SELASSIE

Last Monarch of Ethiopia: Emperor Haile Selassie, called the Lion of Judah, was gently deposed on September 12, 1974.

Background: Haile Selassie claimed to be a descendant of King Solomon and the Queen of Sheba. He ruled the African nation for fifty-seven years, first as regent before becoming emperor. He put an end to slavery in Ethiopia. Forced from his throne at the prelude of World War II with the Italian occupation, he was restored as king in 1941. On August 17, 1975, Haile Selassie died of natural causes at his palace in the Ethiopian capital of Addis Ababa. Born in 1891, he was eighty-three years old.

JIMMY HOFFA

Last Seen: Jimmy Hoffa was last seen in the parking lot of the Machus Red Fox Restaurant in Detroit's Bloomfield township, Michigan, on July 30, 1975.

Background: The former president of the International Brotherhood of Teamsters got into his car at the restaurant at 3:30 in the afternoon and proceeded to drive south on Telegraph Road. He was never seen again. According to the U.S. Justice Department, Hoffa was kidnapped and strangled and his remains were disposed of in a fat-rendering plant, which was later mysteriously destroyed in a fire. Before his disappearance, James Riddle Hoffa was believed to be involved in a power struggle to unseat his former protege, Frank Fitzsimmons, as Teamsters president.

SISAVANG VATTHANA

Last Monarch of Laos: King Sisavang Vatthana abdicated on December 2, 1975, when the Pathet Lao, a Communist independent organization, ousted the coalition government.

Background: The abdication of King Sisavang Vatthana brought to an end a monarchy that went back to 1353. Today Laos is a People's Democratic Republic.

GERALD RUDOLPH FORD

(Thirty-eighth President of the United States)

Last Day in Office: January 20, 1977, after less than one term. Gerald Ford became the thirty-eighth president upon the resignation of Richard Nixon.

Background: Upon taking office, President Ford chose former New York Governor Nelson A. Rockefeller to be his vice president. Remembered as a leader in congress, for stumbling on golf courses, and for being very good-natured, Ford succeeded Vice President Spiro Agnew on October 10, 1973, after Agnew resigned in a kickback scandal. Ford later succeeded President Nixon (August 9, 1974), after Nixon resigned in the face of the Watergate scandal. Ford pardoned Nixon about a month later. He survived two attempts on his life, one by Lynnette "Squeaky" Fromme (1975), another by Sara Jane Moore (1975). His wife, Betty Ford, founded the abuse treatment center that bears her name.

JOHN PAUL I

Last Day of Life: Pope John Paul I died on September 29, 1978.

Background: Awakened at 5 in the morning on September 28, 1978, the pontiff said Mass in his private chapel at 5:30. After Mass, at about 6:15, John Paul I repaired to his chambers in the Apostolic Palace for breakfast and said his Daily Office. At about 8, John Paul I began his workday by receiving ten cardinals from the Philippines. The pope spoke English, occasionally relying on an interpreter. The audience with the cardinals was the first of thirteen audiences on the schedule. The pope broke up the day with a light lunch at noon, followed by a nap.

John Paul I opened his afternoon schedule by acquainting himself with the world situation, scanning half a dozen Italian newspapers, taking note of the Middle East situation and, of great concern to him, the Camp David accords. The pope already knew the Israeli Knesset had approved the peace accords with Egypt and was very pleased by this development. After a private meeting with the cardinal who headed the Congregation of Bishops and an audience with the head of the Melchite rite, John Paul I concluded his working day. His last meal was taken that evening, consisting of some veal, vegetables, salad, and a glass of wine. A meeting with the Vatican secretary of state at 7:30 was his last official duty. After the meeting, John Paul I went to his private chapel for his evening prayers. At 10 the pope prepared for bed. As John Paul I sat in bed reading Thomas à Kempis's *Imitation of Christ,* a phone call from a priest informed him that a leftist student in Rome had been murdered. John Paul I responded with his last words, "Are those young people shooting at each other again? Really, it is terrible."

When the pope failed to appear for his celebration of Mass on Friday morning, September 29, 1978, his secretary, Father Magee, knocked on the pontiff's bedroom door but received no response. The concerned priest went to a window through which he was able to see John Paul I sitting in bed, his lamp burning. Father Magee entered the pope's bedroom, there to behold John Paul I leaning forward, a peaceful smile on his face, in his hands the copy of *Imitation of Christ* still open, indicating that the pontiff had died while reading. The Vatican secretary of state, Cardinal Jean Villet, was immediately summoned. Kneeling at the pope's bedside, the cardinal, attending to the ancient Vatican rite, called the pope three times by his given name: "Albino, Albino, Albino." Rising, the cardinal made the official announcement of the pontiff's passing to those in the room: *"Vere papa Joannes Paulus mortuus est"* ("Pope John Paul is truly dead"). The pope's seal with which John Paul I was invested at his election, the Ring of the Fisherman, was officially broken and destroyed that very day by the chamberlain. John Paul I was the forty-fifth pope to die within a year of installation. Born October 17, 1912, he was sixty-five years old.

MOHAMMED REZA SHAH PAHLAVI

Last Monarch of Iran: Mohammed Reza Shah Pahlavi was ousted from power on February 11, 1979, by followers of the Ayatollah Ruhollah Khomeini, when the shah's military forces capitulated to revolutionary forces.

Background: On January 16, 1979, the shah had left Iran for what was described as a vacation; leaving the nation in the hands of the regency council, he went to Cuernavaca, Mexico. On October 23, 1979, the U.S. State Department made arrangements for the ailing former monarch, age sixty, to enter the United States for what were said to be humanitarian reasons. The shah entered the New York Hospital–Cornell Medical Center, where a series of thorough medical tests revealed gallstones and biopsies of samples taken from his neck showed cancerous tissue. In the meantime, the political atmosphere in the shah's homeland was heating up. His presence in the United States produced a student backlash in Iran that resulted in a takeover of the United States Embassy in Tehran, Iran, on November 4, 1979, and the taking of sixty-six hostages.

On December 3, 1979, Iran approved a new Islamic constitution, officially abolishing the monarchy. With Iran threatening to try the hostages as spies unless the shah was returned, the United States, its honor and integrity at stake, made arrangements for the shah to convalesce in South America after a series of operations to halt the spread of his cancer. After a short stay in Panama, where extradition proceedings to Iran were rumored, the shah fled to Cairo, Egypt, on March 23, 1980, at the invitation of Egyptian President Anwar Sadat. On July 27, 1980, the shah died of cancer in Cairo.

LOUIS MOUNTBATTEN

Last Day of Life: Lord Louis Mountbatten, Earl of Burma, was assassinated on August 27, 1979.

Background: Mountbatten was one of the most revered figures of the British nation, the ideal target for the Provisional IRA to attract attention to its cause of the United Ireland. A dignified, handsome, and genuinely warm and charming man, Mountbatten was a World War II hero. A former governor-general of India, involved in the negotiations with Gandhi for India's eventual peace, he was a cousin of Queen Elizabeth II.

A lover of the outdoors, Mountbatten particularly relished his annual month-long summer holidays at Classiebawn at Donegal in County Silgo, Northwest Ireland. In Ireland, Mountbatten's sterling reputation as an elder statesmen of royal lineage was well known, and residents of the village of Mullaghmore that extends into Donegal Bay, where fishing is a way of life, took pride in Mountbatten's visits. August 27, 1979, promised to be one of the gorgeous days the Irish tourist guides boast of. With great vigor for a man of seventy-nine, Lord Mountbatten in casual dress set out in his *Shadow V* fishing vessel with a royal party consisting of his grandson Nicholas, his daughter Lady Brabourne, and her husband. It was a fitting day to fish and cruise in the bay.

Unknown to the royal party, sometime before they set sail—perhaps the night before as the *Shadow V* was moored, unguarded, at the public dock—IRA bomb specialists had planted a deadly device that could be exploded by remote control. The *Shadow V* idled out in the bay as Lord Mountbatten and his boat boy, Paul Maxwell, age fifteen, inspected lobster pots. Just after 12 noon an explosion broke the serenity. The attention of those on land darted to a flaming destruction that only seconds before had been the *Shadow V* pulling out to bay. Some four boats in the immediate area raced to the tragedy, finding amid the burning debris, the fading, torn figure of Lord Mountbatten, his body half gone. He died before help could arrive. Also killed were Paul Maxwell, Mountbatten's fourteen-year-old grandson Nicholas, and Lady Brabourne, who expired of her injuries at the nearby hospital.

SIXPENCE

Last Minting: The sixpence was last minted in Great Britain on June 30, 1980.

Background: The sixpence went into circulation in 1551 and became known throughout the world through the nursery rhyme:

> *Sing a song of sixpence,*
> *A pocket full of rye.*
> *Four and twenty blackbirds,*
> *Baked in a pie.*

WILLIE SUTTON

Last Day of Life: Willie Sutton died of old age on November 2, 1980, at Spring Hill, Florida. He was seventy-nine years old.

JAMES EARL CARTER, JR

(Thirty-ninth President of the United States)

Last Day in Office: January 20, 1981, after one term.

Background: President Carter introduced such White House austerity measures as turning out unnecessary lights and giving fewer dinner parties. The Carter Administration did not get along well with Congress, and some said Congress was contemptuous of Carter's peanut-farmer background. His greatest success was his sponsorship of the Camp David peace negotiations between Egyptian President Anwar Sadat and Israeli Prime

Minister Menachem Begin in 1978. *Time* magazine named him its Man of the Year in 1976.

ANWAR SADAT

Last Day of Life: Anwar Sadat was assassinated on October 6, 1981.

Background: The Egyptian president was not one to agonize over his safety. He sometimes dismissed his immediate security personnel, feeling they were a nuisance. He was not impressed with the awesome figure that he was as the only moderating force in a region where peace is fragile amid terrorism, small wars, and Islamic fundamentalists crying for a holy war to bury Israel and rid the Mideast of all traces of Western influence. Anwar Sadat died on October 6, 1981, eight years to the day after he, as Egyptian president, surprised Israel by making war against the Jewish state on their high holy day of Yom Kippur. Egypt did not emerge victorious but her national feelings were soothed somewhat, after having been crushed in 1967 in the Six-Day War with Israel that cost Egypt its West Bank of Jordan. Through the Camp David peace accords in 1978, Sadat was getting Egypt back its lost territories. For his work in the Camp David agreement, which called for peace between Egypt and Israel, he shared the Nobel Prize with Israel's leader Menachem Begin. But the accords with the Jewish state cost Sadat Arab friends and made him many enemies, among them Khaled Ahmed Shawki al-Islambouli and the Muslim fanatical group Al Taqfir wal Hijra (Atonement of the Holy Flight)—Islamic fundamentalists who believed the Egyptian leader was drifting away from Islamic principles. Branded a heretic, Sadat was gunned down by four assassins led by Islambouli, most likely with help from inside the Egyptian armed forces.

At noon, on October 6, 1981, in Cairo, Sadat, military leaders, and Egyptian and foreign statesman were witnessing the conclusion of a military parade from a viewing stand. An artillery truck suddenly broke from a vehicle column and stopped in front of the reviewing stand. Perhaps the engine had developed mechanical trouble, thought some of the dignitaries. Sadat's attention at that moment was turned skyward to the Mirage jet fighters overhead. The noise drowned out gunfire from automatic weapons coming from the stalled truck. At the same time, the driver of the truck left his seat and lobbed a hand grenade into the dignitaries, but fortunately it was a dud. The soldiers from the truck boldly approached the reviewing stand, firing into the scattering dignitaries.

Another grenade was thrown and failed to explode, but a third shattered the front of the reviewing stand, sending shrapnel into Sadat's chest and face. Gunfire from three assassins repeatedly struck the president, who had been standing. There was almost no immediate return fire from the guards of the reviewing stand as bullets tore through chairs that were the only protection for guests. Shots from the reviewing stand killed one assassin and wounded the other three. Sadat lay amid strewn chairs, bleeding from the head and mouth. Taken by helicopter to Maadi Hospital, the Egyptian president was dead on arrival.

BEAR BRYANT

Last Game: In the game on December 29, 1982, football coach Bear Bryant led Alabama in a 21–15 victory over Illinois to win the Liberty Bowl. It was Bryant's 323rd win of his college football career. With his 315th win (on January 28, 1981) Bear Bryant surpassed Amos Alonzo Stagg as the winningest college football coach of all time. Bryant took only thirty-seven seasons to achieve that status, while Stagg coached in fifty-seven seasons.

Background: Bear Bryant may not have had the charisma or colorful personality of Knute Rockne, but he is loved and immortalized for his outstanding record of winning 323 college games. Joe Namath, Ken Stabler, and Ray Perkins played under his leadership. Born at Moro Bottom, Arkansas, in 1913, Bryant began his coaching ca-

reer at Alabama as an assistant coach in 1935. After
serving in World War II he returned to college football
coaching—with Maryland State in 1945, Kentucky
though 1953, and Texas A&M through 1957. From 1958
through 1982 he became renowned at Alabama.

Through the years his quarterbacks, tight ends, and
halfbacks went from Alabama to professional football—
players like Richard Todd, Babe Parille, George Blanda,
Steve Sloan, and Bob Baumhower. Others became football college coaches, including Jackie Sherrill, Jerry Glai-
bourne, and Ray Perkins, who headed the New York
Giants before coming home to his alma mater to take
over for the retiring Bear Bryant.

Bear Bryant coached at a time when college football
was severely scrutinized. It was (and still is) a time of big
television contracts and tons of publicity. Though he
had offers to coach elsewhere for more money, he stayed
with Alabama and made the team one of the best in
college football history. He put Alabama on the map,
just as Rockne put Notre Dame on the map, by winning
games. The Bear did it with honor, tapping talent black
and white. Like Rockne, he was a football coach's coach;
as Frank Broyles, former coach of Arkansas, said, "They
don't make them like Bear Bryant anymore," the kind
of coach who wins 323 games in thirty-seven seasons.

MEYER LANSKY

Last Day of Life: On January 15, 1983, at his home in Miami
Beach, Florida, Meyer Lansky, who had outlived all his
criminal friends, died of lung cancer. Born Maier Su-
chowljansky in Grodino, Russia, in 1902, he was eighty-
one years old.

BEAR BRYANT

Last Day of Life: On January 27, 1983, at Tuscaloosa, Alabama, football coach Bear Bryant, died from a heart attack at age sixty-nine.

INDIRA GANDHI

Last Day of Life: India's Prime Minister Indira Gandhi was murdered on October 31, 1984.

Background: The day of reckoning had been set on a June day in 1984 when a holy shrine was violated. On orders from India's Prime Minister Indira Gandhi, military troops sent to the northern state of Punjab, home of India's fourteen million Sikhs, entered the hallowed Golden Temple at Armitsar to root out extremists. The incident resulted in more than six hundred deaths of both Sikhs and soldiers and further riots, and set the stage for a day of infamy—the assassination of Prime Minister Indira Gandhi. The old Sikh prophecy, "When the Golden Temple will be violated, the dynasty will fall," decreed that religion take precedence over civil duty in the hearts of two Sikh guards, Beant Singh and Satwant Singh, members of a five-man security team entrusted with the safety of Indira Gandhi, the "mother" of over seven hundred million people.

On the morning of October 31, 1984, Indira Gandhi emerged from her palace, on her way to meet with British actor Peter Ustinov to continue discussions about film projects. It was a lovely day with soft, cool autumn breezes whipping against Gandhi's bright orange sari as she began to walk from her New Delhi Palace toward a gate where death awaited. With her were three guards and an assistant. To the two Sikh guards, Beant Singh and Satwant Singh, Gandhi spoke her last word, "Namaste" ("Greetings to you"). Having responded, Beant Singh calmly drew his service revolver, a .38 pistol, and fired three shots into the stunned prime minister, who toppled backward from the force of the rounds that pierced her lower stomach. As she crumpled on the ground in pain, Satwant Singh began pouring gunfire upon the fallen leader from an automatic weapon, emptying all thirty rounds into her. As her orange sari quickly became bloodstained, she expired, just two weeks before her sixty-seventh birthday.

RONALD REAGAN
(Fortieth President of the United States)

Last Day in Office: January 20, 1989, after two terms.

Background: Ronald Reagan began his career as a film
actor (appearing in more than fifty movies) and after
becoming a politician, he served as the Governor of California for two terms (1966–1974).

Ronald Reagan liked to smile and wave playfully to
reporters as the helicopter engines sounded loudly on
the White House lawn, drowning out the voices of inquiring reporters. His wife, Nancy, is believed to have
consulted an astrologer in matters concerning traveling
dates—this after an attempt on Reagan's life in 1981.
Reagan initiated sweeping tax reforms and fought for
prayer in the schools. He was a proponent of the pro-
life movement, quipping, "I notice all those that are for
abortion have already been born." Reagan reduced social programs and increased America's defense capabil-
ities. He once said: "I used to say that politics was the
second oldest profession, and I have come to know that
it bears a gross similarity to the first."

BERLIN WALL

Last Day: The end of the Berlin Wall occurred officially at
midnight on October 3, 1990, when East and West Germany were once again united as one Germany after almost fifty years of partition.

Background: The Berlin Wall of Berlin, Germany, was
created between August 15 and 17, 1961, by the East
German Communist government to halt the mass exo-
dus of East Germans fleeing to the West in hopes of a
better life. The Berlin Wall replaced a barbed-wire fence
that had separated East from West Berlin and came in
response to concerns from the Warsaw Pact countries,
worried that the flow of skilled workers fleeing East Germany contributed to an already shaky economy in the

Communist sector. The German border was officially closed on August 13, 1961, on orders from East German head Walter Ulbricht.

The Berlin Wall of solid brick was to become the most significant symbol of what already had become known as the Cold War—a nonshooting war of psychological enmity between the Soviet Union and its bloc nations and the West led by the United States, France, and Great Britain. The Berlin Wall faced its first crisis when on October 26, 1961, East Berlin authorities blocked free passage of U.S. citizens trying to enter East Berlin unmolested at the Friedrichstrasse crossing. Both the United States and the Soviets seemed headed for a confrontation when their tanks moved up to the wall. The Soviets were first to withdraw their tanks, on October 28, and the United States followed suit.

The Berlin Wall extended some twenty-six miles through the heartland of Berlin, following a serpentine course; its chief features were the Brandenburg Gate, marking entry into East Berlin, and Checkpoint Charlie in the American sector at Friedrichstrasse and Zimmerstrasse. The Berlin Wall consisted of steel girders and round-the-clock military manned towers whose soldiers had orders to shoot to kill those seeking to cross either way, east or west. By night brilliant floodlights imitated daylight conditions. There were electrified barbed-wire fences, massive trenches able to swallow whole tanks, heavily mined grounds, and a host of other death traps for freedom-seekers. Many brave East Germans sought to escape to freedom. Some were fortunate, but others were shot dead in full view of West Germans who could do nothing but yell out their rage at the soldiers manning the watchtowers.

Perhaps the most famous event concerning the Berlin Wall occurred on June 26, 1963, when President John F. Kennedy, on a four-day visit to Germany, stood at the wall and, before a mass of over one million West Germans, declared, *"Ich bin ein Berliner"* ("I am a Berliner").

COLD WAR

Last Day: After almost fifty years, the last day of the Cold War was marked by the reunification of East and West Germany at the stroke of midnight on October 3, 1990. The symbol of the Cold War—the Berlin Wall, cutting off free access between East and West Germany—was no more.

Background: At the Conference of Yalta on February 4–11, 1945, attended by President Roosevelt, Winston Churchill, and Joseph Stalin, the Big Four powers, Great Britain, France, the United States, and the Soviet Union, had settled on agreements to occupy the defeated German nation. Germany was to be divided among the four powers, each to occupy one zone. A few months later at the Potsdam Conference the final details of the Allied occupation—a set of guiding principles—were hammered out. The settlements of Germany by the Allies were not to be permanent. When peace and stability had been fully restored, a peace treaty would be made with Germany, with the principal aim of reuniting the country.

But hardly had the ink dried on the agreements when problems arose that would result in the Cold War. Joseph Stalin and the Soviet Union were unhappy with the settlement terms at Yalta even though he agreed to them at Yalta and Potsdam. The Soviet Union had second thoughts concerning postwar German reparations, the nature and the extent of what she would receive, and the industrial output that Germany would be allowed to achieve. Stalin was determined to prevent the resurrection of German aggressive power. This last factor was a legitimate concern for twenty million of her people had died in the war at the hands of the Nazis; she had paid a great price. Stalin also believed Russian participation ultimately brought about Germany's defeat.

The Marshall Plan to rebuild war-torn Europe was unacceptable to the Soviet Union because it ran counter to socialization and collectivization, vital tenets of Marxism; the plan was a prescription for eventual prosperity through private enterprise by the participants. Stalin was also disturbed by the American presence in Europe. He once told a Czech official that "the aim of Soviet policy was to get the Americans out of Europe and Asia." Mainly in Eastern Europe, some nations fell under Soviet domination and were called Soviet bloc countries: East Germany, Romania, Poland, Albania, Bulgaria, Hungary, and Czechoslovakia. Under the Warsaw Pact of November 1954, in response to the creation of the North Atlantic Treaty Organization (NATO) in 1949, these Soviet bloc nations would defend the Soviet Union and themselves from the West, mainly the United States. The Soviets gained an atomic bomb in 1947 and began an arms race, giving rise to what became known as the Cold War.

Throughout the succeeding years the Cold War would be waged by the Soviet Union with a series of aggressions, among these the crushing of an uprising in Hungary on October 23, 1956; the building of the Berlin Wall between East and West Germany on August 13, 1961 to stop Germans from leaving East Germany; the initiation of the Cuban Missile Crisis on October 22, 1962, while supporting a Communist regime in Cuba; the support of the North Vietnamese and Vietcong during the Vietnam War from 1964 to 1973; the invasion of Czechoslovakia on August 20, 1968; and the invasion of Afghanistan on December 27, 1979.

At Yalta, the intriguing "German question" had been raised. What would be the future of Germany? The Cold War had its roots in the German question, and a wall in that country became its symbol. Fittingly, in that same country, most of the world would find true peace when that symbol was at last dissolved, bringing about one Germany. Boris Yeltsin, head of Russia, declared at Camp David in meetings with U.S. President George Bush on February I, 1992: "The concept of America as an enemy has been removed from Russian military doctrine." A new age, one of peace, has been born between the United States and the Russian Commonwealth of States.

WARSAW PACT

Last Day: The last day of the Warsaw Treaty Organization, or Warsaw Pact, was April 1, 1991, when the Soviet parliament called for the military organization's complete demise. Within hours of the Soviet mandate, the Warsaw Pact was dissolved.

Background: Established late in 1954, the Warsaw Treaty Organization was a military alliance of the Soviet bloc countries that became popularly known as the Warsaw Pact after its signing in Warsaw, Poland. The Warsaw Pact was established by the Soviet Union in response to the Western powers' Paris Pact in 1954, which allowed West Germany to embark on a limited rearmament program and to join the North Atlantic Treaty Organization (NATO). The Warsaw Pact was the Soviet answer to NATO, the defense shield of Western free Europe established in 1949. The Warsaw Pact was designed to thwart aggression by the West by providing a collective defense against NATO; and as with NATO, an attack on any Warsaw Pact nation was an attack against them all. The Warsaw Pact countries consisted of Poland, Albania (which withdrew in 1965), Bulgaria, Czechoslovakia, East Germany, Hungary, Romania, and the Soviet Union. Its headquarters were in Moscow. Warsaw Pact countries moved against both Hungary (1956) and Czechoslovakia (1968), considering those countries to be under anti-Communist elements who sought to undermine their Communist regimes. With the end of the Warsaw Pact, new freedoms had begun to pervade the countries of Eastern Europe, no longer Soviet bloc nations. With the dissolution of the Soviet Union on December 26, 1991, the countries of Eastern Europe were able to pursue their own destinies.

GULF WAR

Last Day: On April 6, 1991, Iraqi President Saddam Hussein accepted the peace terms for his defeated nation. Among the terms reluctantly agreed to by the president as stipulated by the United Nations, Iraq was to renounce terrorism, pay billions in war reparations to Kuwait, permit the destruction of her chemical and biological weapons, surrender her atomic weapons and materials connected with her nuclear arsenal, destroy her Scud and other missiles, and confine herself to her own borders as dictated by the United Nations before the August 2, 1990, invasion of Kuwait.

Background: The Persian Gulf War began to take shape on August 2, 1990, when news broke across the world that President Saddam Hussein of Iraq had invaded the sovereign territory of his neighbor, oil-rich Kuwait, attacking and overrunning the military and civilian authority. Saddam's motives were twofold: to gain control of billions in oil revenues that Kuwait realized annually, and to gain access to a deepwater port on the Persian Gulf. In a terrible miscalculation, Saddam Hussein did not realize that the world would do more than mouth diplomatic protests, it would go to war against him. When the war had ended, Iraq sacrificed an estimated one hundred thousand of her people, her major city of Baghdad was left in shambles, and her foreign bank accounts were frozen. She had suffered a strangling embargo and sanctions, and had been condemned by the United Nations—member countries had participated in a coalition of money, troops, armor, and medical personnel to soundly defeat her.

Coalition nations included Afghanistan, Argentina, Australia, Bahrain, Bangladesh, Belgium, Canada, Czechoslovakia, Denmark, Egypt, France, Greece, Hungary, Italy, Japan, Kuwait, Morocco, the Netherlands, New Zealand, Nigeria, Norway, Oman, Pakistan, Poland, the Philippines, Qatar, Romania, Saudi Arabia, Senegal, Sierra Leone, Singapore, South Korea, Spain, Sweden, Syria, the United Arab Emirates, and the United States. The Allied commander was U.S. General Norman Schwarzkopf. Iraq received moral support from the Palestine Liberation Organization and King Hussein of Jordan, whose people supported Iraq. The Soviet Union eventually sided with the United States in the dispute; she sent no troops.

The war took billions of dollars to finance, with Saudi Arabia, Kuwait, Japan, and West Germany being chief contributors.

On August 6, 1990, four days after Iraq invaded Kuwait, the United Nations had ordered a trade and financial boycott against Iraq, and on August 7, President Bush launched Operation Desert Shield. Shortly afterward the United States formed a coalition of nations to redress the Iraq invasion of Kuwait. With war imminent, thousands of guest workers fled Iraq, spilling into its neighbor Jordan, creating a refugee problem that resulted in Jordan closing her borders. In the chaos, Saddam Hussein took some Western hostages, whom he eventually released. In the meantime, because of panic buying, oil prices shot up from the benchmark price of $18 to $40 a barrel.

Negotiations were under way among Iraq, the United States, and the Soviet Union with no progress being made. Under Desert Shield, the United States and coalition countries began a massive buildup of troops and armor in the Persian Gulf and initiated a naval blockade of Iraq, preventing shiploads of arms or oil tankers from leaving or entering Iraq or Kuwait. Iraq, in the face of world condemnation, bolstered its troop force in Kuwait by 250,000 men.

On November 29, 1990, the United States approved Resolution 678 calling for Iraq to withdraw from Kuwait by January 15, 1991, or face military ouster by coalition forces. Coalition forces continued arriving in Saudi Arabia, and by January 12 numbered almost four hundred thousand troops, with tens of thousands of pieces of fighting equipment, from tanks to armored personnel carriers to all manner of weaponry, including rockets, rocket launchers, howitzers, escort fuel and supply trucks, gas masks, and night vision equipment. On January 12, 1991, Congress in a close vote authorized President Bush to go to war. Iraq's parliament shortly after rubber-stamped Saddam Hussein's wishes to fight a war.

On January 15, 1991, the world sensed something terrible in the wind, but nothing happened. On January 17 (January 18 in Iraq), as most Americans were occupied with the dinner hour, Desert Storm began. Saddam promised it would be the "mother of all battles." Television viewers across the world saw the skies over Baghdad ablaze with antiaircraft fire, the likes of which had not been seen since World War II. Stealth bombers and Cruise missiles knocked out Iraq's key telecommunication centers. In the next four days, round-the-clock bombing thundered over both Iraq and Kuwait as jets from land bases and carriers—more than two thousand strong—saturated specified targets.

There was no let-up after the initial four-day bombardment, with Iraq's air force almost totally incapacitated. U.S., British, and French pilots led in the air strikes, with Saudi Arabia, Canada, and South Korea also providing pilots. The air strikes mounted into the thousands, with command and control centers taking devastating hits. Air bases were bombed, their runways pitted with deep craters. Nuclear facilities and arms manufacturing plants took salvos, as did roads, bridges, electrical facilities, water plants, and public and government buildings. Within a five-week period from the start of Desert Storm, coalition sorties (single flights by a single aircraft) numbered over one hundred thousand, with payloads in excess of almost ninety thousand tons of explosives. The most feared of all weapons were the giant B-52 bombers that pounded Iraq's desert positions and with heavy fire prepared the way for a limited ground war.

Iraq, in an effort to persuade Syria to break with the coalition, launched Scud missiles at Israel, in hopes she would enter the war, having to violate Jordan's air space to inflict retaliatory strikes. It did not work. Israel stayed put, depending on the security of the U.S. Patriot missiles to intercept the Scuds.

To add to the woes of the conflict, Saddam Hussein unleashed an ecological nightmare when his forces willfully let Kuwait oil spill into the gulf, destroying fish and wildlife. An oil slick from the gulf threatened to destroy Saudi Arabia's water supply.

On February 25 a Scud missile scored a direct hit on an American barracks in Dhahran, Saudi Arabia, killing twenty-eight Americans. Less than two weeks before, on February 13, Saddam Hussein scored points in the propaganda war when U.S. planes bombed what they believed was a military target but in fact turned out to be a civilian air-raid shelter; 334 men, women, and children lost their lives. With the ferocity of the conflict increasing, coalition forces were equipped with special clothing and gas masks against Iraq's chemical and biological weapons, which were never used. U.S. planes from B-52s to F-15s had almost outlived their usefulness as troops had either surrendered, or remained in their bunkers waiting for the inevitable ground war, which began on February 23.

By February 28, the ground war was over. The elite Iraqi Republican Guard was hardly heard from except for one tank battle in which the Republican Guard broke off the engagement by fleeing back across the border into Iraq in what had been a fierce tank battle. On February 28 Kuwait was liberated. The Iraqi army upon leaving Kuwait had set over four hundred oil wells ablaze, filling the air for miles with thick, noxious black smoke that turned midday into night. They also left behind thousands of mines to further kill and maim. The liberated country had been totally ravaged, its buildings leveled, its goods of every kind carted off to Iraq, including the traffic lights. Out in the desert, tired, tattered, fearful, and famished, Iraqi soldiers were surrendering by the thousands. For hundreds of square miles, the work of the B-52s and other planes was in evidence as the desert was littered with burned-out tanks, trucks, and other armored vehicles, including buses that housed the charred remains of enemy soldiers.

Throughout the entire war the world watched daily press briefings from Saudi Arabia via satellite, showing actual footage of air strikes as filmed by cameras fitted to planes. The footage presented a vivid picture of the Gulf War. Television networks preempted regularly scheduled programs to cover the war. Iraq's losses were estimated to be over one hundred thousand dead, three hundred thousand wounded. Coalition fatalities were placed at under just three hundred men and women, including deaths from so-called friendly fire.

In the aftermath of the war, an unexpected refugee problem occurred when a million Kurds fled Iraq in fear of persecutions by Saddam Hussein. They were to become wards of the world. Iraq was reduced to less than a Third World country as its industry, technology, communication systems, schools, businesses, farms, bridges, and reservoirs were destroyed, and its leaders were reviled by the world. But Saddam Hussein—the man who brought the spotlight of the world to his doorstep and took his country through two costly wars within ten years of his presidency, the man who had to pay billions in reparations to the country he stole from, the man who polluted the Gulf and brought his nation sorrow—was still in power.

BALTIC COUNTRIES

Last Day As Part of the Soviet Union: Estonia, Latvia, and Lithuania became independent on September 6, 1991.

Background: Estonia officially broke away from the Soviet Union when she was granted her complete independence on September 6, 1991. Recognized by the United States and other powers as a sovereign nation— officially the Republic of Estonia—she is a member of the United Nations. Estonia was annexed by the Soviet Union in 1940 in a secret pact with Adolf Hitler and Joseph Stalin; this secret pact was viewed as illegal by Estonia and was at the root of her quest for independence. She fell into German hands briefly after but was retaken by the Soviet Union in 1944. Population: 1.6 million. She is culturally related to Finland.

Latvia won her complete independence from the Soviet Union on September 5, 1991. Her sovereignty was recognized by the United States and other major powers. Officially the Republic of Latvia, she is a member of the United Nations. Formerly in the Soviet fold, before World War II Latvia objected to the secret Hitler-Stalin pact that incorporated her into the Soviet Union in

1939, and on the basis of the nonaggression pact, which she claimed was illegal, sought her independence. Latvia was overrun by Germany in 1941 and retaken by the Soviets in 1944. Population: 2.7 million.

Lithuania declared her complete independence and won it on September 6, 1991, her sovereignty recognized by the United States and other major powers. Officially the Republic of Lithuania, she is a member of the United Nations. Having signed a mutual assistance pact with the Soviet Union in 1940, Lithuania was overrun by Germany in 1941, but retaken by the Russian army in 1944. Her annexation by the Soviet Union was viewed as illegal and was at the root of her struggle for independence. Population: 3.7 million.

The new freedom at last realized by the Baltic republics will make them responsible for their own destinies. They have become self-governing democracies.

UNION OF SOVIET SOCIALIST REPUBLICS

Last Day: The end of the USSR, or Soviet Union, occurred officially on December 26, 1991, after seventy-four years of existence.

Background: When the Supreme Soviet voted itself out of existence, the Soviet Union officially passed into history. In its place was born a Commonwealth of Independent States, as decided by Russian Federation President Boris Yeltsin and Ukraine President Leonid Kravchuk on December 8, 1991. The members of the Commonwealth of Independent States are Russia, Ukraine, Byelorussia, Tadzhikistan, Kirghizia, Kazakhstan, Armenia, Azerbaidzhan, Moldavia, Turkmenistan, and Uzbekistan.

The Soviet Union had begun in 1917 with the Russian Revolution that brought Vladimir Ilyich Ulyanov Lenin to power after the brutal ouster of the Russian monarchy. Russia was torn by civil war, from 1918 to 1920, between the Bolshevik Communists, or Reds (because of the color of their flag), and the Whites, former czarist officers and upper classes of Russian society. The White army was supported by the United States, Great Britain, and France. The Bolsheviks eventually triumphed over the White forces after receiving support from patriotic Russians who resented foreign interference in Russian affairs; many Russian peasants feared that if the Whites won the civil war, the Russian monarchy might return and the old powerful landlords might be reinstated.

By 1923 the USSR was founded. By the end of World War II it consisted of fifteen republics: Russia, Ukraine, Byelorussia, Tadzhikistan, Kirghizia, Kazakhstan, Armenia, Azerbaidzhan, Moldavia, Turkmenistan, Uzbekistan, Georgia, Estonia, Latvia, and Lithuania.

With the death of Lenin on January 21, 1924, Joseph Stalin took control of the Communist Party. After a power struggle in which Stalin eliminated his enemies and forced one of the founders of the Soviet state, Leon Trotsky, to flee the country (Trotsky would later be assassinated by Stalin's agent on August 21, 1940), Stalin was firmly in control of Soviet Russia.

Joseph Stalin became a cruel dictator who seized the peasants' lands as he embarked on a series of five-year plans to get Russia back on its feet. Many of the wealthy peasants (called Kulaks, after the nineteenth-century wealthy peasant class) objected to giving up their lands in the Stalinist collectivization farm programs, killing their livestock and burning their farms. With a vengeance, Stalin began his terrible purges in which millions of peasants were murdered or sent to Siberian starvation camps where they perished from the elements. By 1934 the peasants had given in, and by 1938 some half a million farms throughout the Soviet Union were under the Soviet collectivization program or were state-owned. In 1936 Stalin believed he had achieved the first phase of Communism—a "nation of workers and peasants," as found in Article 1 of the newly drawn up Soviet Constitution.

After World War II, in which Russia was to lose some twenty million people to the Germans, Stalin was able to bargain for land after his participation on the side of the Allies helped defeat the Nazis. At Yalta in 1945 Stalin was able to spread his power base beyond Soviet borders when the USSR was allowed to occupy part of Germany. With Winston Churchill's Iron Curtain speech warning of Russian expansion in 1946, a Russian blockade of Berlin on April 1, 1948, its objection to the Marshall Plan of June 5, 1947–January 1, 1952, and its eventual acquisition of the atomic bomb in 1947, a Cold War had begun—a nonshooting aggression between the United States, Great Britain, France, and West Germany, and the Soviet Union.

With the death of Stalin on March 5, 1953, Nikita Khrushchev emerged as the head of the Communist Party. He fared no better than Stalin in getting the Russian economy off the ground, as his farm programs were a dismal failure, resulting in the Soviet Union having to purchase grain from the West. Khrushchev increased East-West tension by authorizing the building of the Berlin Wall on August 13, 1961, cutting off freedom of access between East and West Germany. Khrushchev also brought missiles to Cuba, aimed at United States, inciting the Cuban Missile Crisis of October 22, 1962. He backed down and removed the missiles.

After Khrushchev was forced out of power in 1964, Leonid Brezhnev became head of the Communist Party. Under Brezhnev, Russia suffered stagnation. The Communist leader sent troops to invade Czechoslovakia on August 20, 1968, and Afghanistan on December 27, 1979. However, under Brezhnev detente began, with its summits with Western leaders and arms control treaties. But the Soviet Union could offer its people little hope as stores lacked sufficient goods, and long lines for such basic staples as bread and milk became a daily fact of life.

With the death of Brezhnev, minor premiers came to power until March 11, 1985, when Mikhail Gorbachev was elected Communist Party chief. Without knowing it, Gorbachev brought about the end of the Soviet Union. He embarked on a philosophy of "restructuring" the Soviet Union, to become known as perestroika, and an openness that became known as glasnost. Glasnost was a success, perestroika was not. Soviet dissidents were freed from prisons, freedom of assembly, speech, and religion was permitted, and arms control agreements with the West were largely successful. In 1988 after Gorbachev was elected president, the Soviet Union pulled out of Afghanistan on April 15, 1988. Soviet bloc nations, including East Germany found their freedom from the Soviet yoke; the Warsaw Pact was eventually disbanded on April 1, 1991; the Berlin Wall fell on October 3, 1990; and the Baltic republics of the Soviet Union—Latvia, Estonia, and Lithuania—won their independence on September 6, 1991.

But the Soviet economy was worsening, with bread lines longer than ever and riots beginning to take hold as dissatisfaction with Gorbachev's economic reforms spread. A coup by Kremlin conservatives to overthrow Gorbachev on August 19, 1991, failed. But shortly thereafter a charismatic opponent to Gorbachev's policies, Boris Yeltsin, having won the presidency of Russia in open elections, gained favor with Russians. Gorbachev's power began to erode. As republic after republic declared its independence from the Soviet Union, a commonwealth of former Soviet republics was born on December 8, 1991. With the resignation of Mikhail Gorbachev on December 26, 1991, and the descending of the red flag with its hammer and sickle on that same day, the Union of Soviet Socialist Republics or Soviet Union, at age seventy-four, had expired.

As voted by the Russian Congress of People's Deputies, as of April 17, 1992, the country of Russia is officially known by the names: Russia, and the Russian Federation.

SOVIET LEADERS SINCE 1917

Prince Georgi Lvov and Alexander Kerensky (1917)
Vladimir Ilyich Lenin (1917–1924)
Aleksei Rykov (1924–1930)
Vyacheslav Molotov (1930–1941)
Joseph Stalin (1941–1953)
Georgi M. Malenkov (1953–1955)

Nikolai A. Bulganin (1955–1958)

Nikita Khrushchev (1958–1964)

Leonid I. Brezhnev (1964–1982)

Yuri V. Andropov (1982–1984)

Konstantin U. Chernenko (1984–1985)

Mikhail S. Gorbachev (1985–1991)

SLOVENIA, CROATIA AND BOSNIA-HERZEGOVINA

Last Day As Part of Yugoslavia: The Republics of Slovenia, Croatia, and Bosnia-Herzegovina were part of Yugoslavia on April 6, 1992. The next day they became sovereign nations, officially recognized by the United States, already having won recognition from the European Community when they previously declared independence.

Background: With the loss of Slovenia, Croatia, and Bosnia-Herzegovina, Yugoslavia, once made up of six republics, now consists of two republics, Serbia and Montenegro. The sixth, Macedonia, declared her independence from Yugoslavia on September 9, 1991, and is expected to win full recognition from both the European Community and the United States, but that is being delayed out of deference to neighboring Greece, who also has a region named Macedonia.

Yugoslavia was so named in 1929 when the Kingdom of the Serbs, Croats, and Slovenes was born, with the proclamation of King Aleksandr I as dictator on October 3, 1929. What became known as Yugoslavia was, before World War I, a patchwork of states that extended from the future Yugoslavia to the lands of the Black Sea, known as the Balkan states. On October 9, 1934, Aleksandr I was assassinated while on a state visit to France. He was succeeded by his son, Peter II, with Prince Paul acting as regent. With the onslaught of World War II, Prince Paul signed an agreement with Germany to join the Axis Alliance on March 25, 1941, but two days later he was overthrown in a coup. Peter II, age seventeen, was installed in Prince Paul's place, with Yugoslavia's air force chief of staff, General Simovic, holding the actual power of the nation. On April 6, 1941, the Nazis invaded the country, forcing Peter II and his government to flee. Two groups of freedom fighters arose to do battle with the Nazis, most significantly the Partisans, composed of Communists and non-Serbians and led by Josef Broz Tito. In 1943 Tito was able to establish a provisional government. In 1945, opposed by those loyal to the monarchy, Tito nevertheless, with the support of both Winston Churchill and Joseph Stalin, won the election to head Yugoslavia as prime minister, proclaiming the nation the Federal People's Republic of Yugoslavia. The monarchy was officially abolished. Tito eventually broke with the Soviets and embarked on a nonaligned policy between the Soviets and the United States. He also kept peace between the Serbian majority in his country and other multiple nationalities—some twenty distinct groups, in addition to Serbians and Croatians, that make up the various republics. With Tito's death on May 4, 1980, the country was governed by a rotating presidency among the six Yugoslavian republics. In 1990 the various nationalities—Eastern Orthodox, Muslim Slavs, and Roman Catholic Croats—entered into a civil war, to some extent triggered by the independence fever that has swept the Soviet bloc as Serbs attempted to crush Muslim Slavs and their Croatian allies, principally in the latest breakaway republic of Bosnia-Herzegovina. If Serbia, whose leaders are old hard-line Communist generals, is allowed to commit aggression against her neighbors without being checked by the United States and Germany, Serbia could create lasting instability in that region, much as Iraq did in the Middle East. Because the region is surrounded by such countries as Austria, Hungary, Romania, and Italy across the Adriatic Sea, restoring peace there is vital.

In March 1992, fifteen hundred United Nations troops entered Yugoslavia as a peace-keeping force. On September 22, 1992, the United States Security Council voted to expel Serbia and Montenegro from the United Nations. And on October 22, 1992, Amnesty International cited Serbia and Montenegro for committing atrocities against Bosnia-Herzegovina by conducting death camps with mass executions.

The countries of Croatia, Slovenia, and Bosnia-Herzegovina, former Yugoslav republics, were officially accepted as new member countries in the United Nations on May 22, 1992.

GEORGE H. BUSH

(Forty-first President of the United States)

Last Day In Office: January 20, 1993, after one term in office.

Background: President Bush assisted in bringing an end to the Cold War. Other successes included the American victory in the Persian Gulf War against Iraq, improving relations with new republics of the former Soviet Union, and the reunification of East and West Germany. At home, George Bush was not as successful. Bush raised taxes, even after promising during his run for the presidency not to do so, telling the public to "Read My Lips. No New Taxes." His critics said he was aloof to the plight of the poor and the growing concerns of the middle class. But President Bush's biggest problem was the nation's economy, which became mired in a recession during his watch.

Bibliography

Abbott, Walter M., S.J. *The Documents of Vatican II*, Guild Press, American Press, Association Press, 1966.

Banks, Ed Arthur S. *Political Handbook of the World*, CSA Publishers, 1981-1990.

Berliner, Barbara with Melinda Corey and George Ochos. *The Book of Answers*, Prentice Hall Press, 1990.

Bronrigg, Ronald. *Who's Who in the New Testament*, Pillar Books, 1971.

Brusher, Joseph S., S.J. *Popes Through the Ages*, D. Van Nostrand Company, Inc., 1959.

Budge, E. A. Wallis. *A Short History of the Egyptian People with Chapters on Their Region, Daily Life, etc.*, J. M. Dent, 1914.

Cartwright, Fredrich F. with Michael D. Biddiss. *Disease and History: The Influence of Disease in Shaping the Great Events of History*, Thomas Y. Crowell, 1972.

Carey, John, Ed. *Eyewitness to History*, Harvard University Press, 1988; Ann Books, 1990.

Cattan, Bruce. *The American Heritage Picture History of the Civil War*, American Heritage, 1960.

Chronicle of the 20th Century, Chronicle Publishers, 1987.

Chronicle of the World, Ecam Publishers, 1989.

Concise Dictionary of American Biography, Scribners & Sons, 1977.

Cook, Denys. *Presidents of the U.S.A.*, Newton Abbot, Devon Publishers, 1981.

Cornell, James. *Great International Disaster Book*, Scribner & Sons, 1982.

Editors of Hamlyn Publishers. *The Monster Book of Questions and Answers*, Hamlyn Publishers, 1989.

Ferrell, Arthur. *The Fall of the Roman Empire*, Thames and Hudson, 1986.

Flexner, Stuart Berg. *I Hear America Talking*, Simon & Schuster, 1979.

Forbes, Malcolm. *They Went That-a Way*, Simon & Schuster, 1988.

Gibbon, Edward. *The History of the Decline and Fall of the Roman Empire*, AMS Press, 1976.

Gipe, George. *The Great American Sports Book*, Dolphin Books, 1978.

Grant, Michael. *Cleopatra*, Weidenfield and Nicholson, 1972.

Grun, Bernard. *The Timetable of History: A Horizontal Linkage of People and Events*, Simon & Schuster, 1975.

Haigh, W.E. *An Analytical Outline of English History*, Oxford University Press, 1924.

Kane, Joseph Nathan. *Facts About the Presidents*, H. W. Wilson Company, 1974.

Keegan, John and Andrew Wheatcroft. *Who's Who in Military History*, Weidenfield and Nicholson, 1976.

Kennedy, John F. *Profiles in Courage*, Harper Publishers, 1957.

Kennedy, Paul. *The Rise and Fall of the Great Powers*, Vintage, 1987.

Macleau, Michael. *The Ten Thousand Day War Vietnam*, St. Martin's Press, 1981.

McElroy, Richard L. *American Presidents and Fascinating Facts, Stories and Questions of Our Chief Executive and Their Families*, Daring Books, 1984.

Marsh, Henry. *The Caesars: The Roman Empire and Its Rulers*, Newton, Abbot, David and Charles Publishers, 1971.

Martin, Louis J. and Associated. *The Book of Facts and Records*, Harbor House, 1977.

Mason, David. *Who's Who in World War I*, Weidenfield and Nicholson, 1979.

Morison, Samuel Eliot. *The Oxford History of the American People*, Oxford University Press, 1965.

Nash, Jay Robert. *Among the Missing: An Anecdotal History of Missing Persons from 1800 to the Present*, Simon & Schuster, 1978.

————. *Bloodletters and Badmen*, Warner Books, 1982.

Olmstead, A.T., *History of the Persian Empire*, University of Chicago Press, 1948.

Palmer, R.R. *Twelve Who Ruled: The Year of Terror in the French Revolution*, Princeton, 1970.

Pearson, John. *Arena: The Story of the Colosseum*, McGraw Hill, 1973.

Reed, Bruce. *Macmillan Concise Dictionary of World History*, Vintage, 1960.

Reed, John. *The Days That Shook the World*, Vintage, 1960.

Sanders, Jonathan. *Russia 1917: The Unpublished Revolution*, Abbeville Press, Inc., 1989.

Schlesinger, Arthur. *The Almanac of American History*, Putnam, 1983.

Shook, Robert L. *The Book of Why*, Hammond, 1983.

Van Der Kemp, Gerald. *Versailles*, Park Lane, 1981.

Wacker, John. *The Roman Empire,* J. M. Dent Publishers, 1987.

Whitney, David C. *The American Presidents,* Doubleday, 1982.

Wills, Garry. *Roman Culture: Weapons and the Man,* George Braziller, 1961.

Index